Read to Succeed 1

Read to Succeed 1

ACADEMIC READING RIGHT FROM THE START

Roberto E. Robledo
Santa Barbara City College

Dolores Howard
Santa Barbara City College

▲

Houghton Mifflin Company
Boston · New York

▼

Publisher: Patricia A. Coryell
Director of ESL Publishing: Susan Maguire
Senior Development Editor: Kathy Sands Boehmer
Editorial Assistant: Evangeline Bermas
Senior Project Editor: Kathryn Dinovo
Senior Manufacturing Coordinator: Marie Barnes
Marketing Manager: Annamarie Rice
Marketing Associate: Laura Hemrika

Cover image: CSA Images © 2003

Photo credits **p. 1:** Roger Smith / Index Stock Imagery; AP / Wide World Photos; © Dennis MacDonald / PhotoEdit; © Bill Aron / PhotoEdit. **p. 2:** Arthur Tilley / Getty Images. **p. 24:** © Frank Siteman / PhotoEdit; © Dennis MacDonald / PhotoEdit; © Spencer Grant / PhotoEdit; Erin Patrice O'Brien / Getty Images. **p. 39:** © Amy Etra / PhotoEdit. **p. 40:** Gary Conner / Index Stock Imagery. **p. 55:** © Michael Newman / PhotoEdit; Bill Bachmann / Index Stock Imagery; © Elena Rooraid / PhotoEdit; © IT Int'l / eStock Photo / PictureQuest. **p. 70:** © Tom McCarthy / PhotoEdit. **p. 87:** Ryan McVay / Getty Images. **p. 88:** © Mary Kate Denny / PhotoEdit. **p. 105:** © Richard Lord / PhotoEdit. **p. 121:** © Strauss/Curtis /CORBIS. **p. 137:** © Michael Newman / PhotoEdit. **p. 138:** © Michael Newman / PhotoEdit. **p. 154:** © John Neubauer / PhotoEdit. **p. 173:** © David Young-Wolff / PhotoEdit. **p. 193:** © Bob Daemmrich / PhotoEdit.

Printed in the U.S.A.

Library of Congress Control Number: 2002109662

ISBN: 0-618-32470-4

123456789-CRS-08 07 06 05 04

Contents

Reading and Skills Chart ix

Introduction xi

Unit 1: Our New Country and School

Chapter 1: Our New Home

Reading 1 Ali's Letter to Mustafa 2

Before You Read 2

Reading 2 Ali's Letter to Mustafa (continued) 8

Before You Read 8

▶ *Grammar Hints: There is / there are* 10

Reading 3 Ali's Letter to Mustafa (six months later) 13

Before You Read 13

Expansion Activities

Activity 1: Make a Family Tree 18

Activity 2: Write a Letter to Your Classmate 20

Chapter 2: Life in the United States

Reading 1 Immigrants in the United States 24

Before You Read 24

Reading 2 A New Life 31

Before You Read 31

▶ *Grammar Hints:* Possessive adjectives 36

Expansion Activities

Activity 1: Use a Map 36

Activity 2: Write about Your Life 37

Unit 2: Study Skills and College Success

Chapter 3: What Interesting Classes!

Reading 1 Colleges and Degrees in the United States 40

Before You Read 40

Reading 2 After ESL 47

Before You Read 47

Expansion Activity

Activity: What's in Your Future? 53

Chapter 4: How to Study English

Reading 1 How to Study and Learn English 56

Before You Read 56

Reading 2 The Dictionary 64

Before You Read 64

Expansion Activities

Activity 1: Record Homework Contacts 68

Activity 2: Practice a Message for Your Teacher 68

Activity 3: Write a Short Letter in English 68

Chapter 5: I Don't Have Time!

Reading 1 Ana's Busy Life 70

Before You Read 70

Reading 2 A Realistic Schedule 79

Before You Read 79

▶ *Grammar Hints:* Present tense 82

Expansion Activities

Activity 1: Time Flies 83

Activity 2: Where Does the Day Go? 84

Activity 3: Time to Relax 85

Unit 3: Survival and Culture

Chapter 6: An Appointment with the Doctor

Reading 1 A Bigger Family for the Itos 88

Before You Read 88

Reading 2 The Physical Examination 97

Before You Read 97

▶ *Grammar Hints:* Object pronouns 102

Expansion Activities

Activity 1: Call the Doctor? 103

Activity 2: What to Do? 103

Chapter 7: There Are Problems in My House

Reading 1 Family Problems 106

Before You Read 106

> ▸ *Grammar Hints:* Present progressive 113

Reading 2 We Have to Leave 114

Before You Read 114

Expansion Activities

Activity 1: What Happens Next? 118

Activity 2: Write and Present a Dialogue 119

Chapter 8: Dating and Holidays in the United States

Reading 1 I Want to Date Her 121

Before You Read 121

Reading 2 Why Do Americans Wear Green on March 17? 126

Before You Read 126

> ▸ *Grammar Hints:* More practice with object pronouns 133

Expansion Activities

Activity 1: Write a Valentine Note 134

Activity 2: Make That Call! 134

Unit 4: Careers, Counseling, and Community

Chapter 9: Looking for a Job

Reading 1 A Layoff 138

Before You Read 138

Reading 2 The Interview 146

Before You Read 146

Expansion Activities

Activity 1: Choose a Job for Olivia 152

Activity 2: Time for an Interview! 152

Chapter 10: What Careers Should I Think About?

Reading 1 Careers and Money 154

Before You Read 154

> ▸ *Grammar Hints: Be + going to + infinitive* for the future 162

Reading 2 Careers for the Future 164

Before You Read 164

Expansion Activity

Activity: The Longer You Go to School 170

Chapter 11: Personal and Family Counseling

Reading 1 A Professional Counselor's Job 173

Before You Read 173

    ▶ *Grammar Hints:* Asking and answering questions in the simple past 178

Reading 2 "Not Me! Well, Maybe . . ." 183

Before You Read 183

    ▶ *Grammar Hints:* Regular past tense 190

Expansion Activity

Activity: Create a Counseling Dialogue 191

Chapter 12: The Community

Reading 1 A New Kind of Assignment 193

Before You Read 193

Reading 2 ESL Students in the Community 204

Before You Read 204

    ▶ *Grammar Hints:* Irregular past tense 210

Expansion Activity

Activity: Where Can I Volunteer? 210

Appendix 213

Reading and Skills Chart

Chapter	Reading Focus	Practical Focus	Grammar Focus	Expansion Activities
1. Our New Home	Comprehension: picture-word association, true-false, sentence completion, graph practice, matching Vocabulary: words in context	Writing letters back to the old country	There is / there are	Make a family tree (describing family members) Write a letter to your classmate (addressing an envelope and writing a letter)
2. Life in the United States	Comprehension: true-false, questions, matching Vocabulary: antonyms, word identification, matching	School and job vocabulary	Possessive adjectives	Use a map (mark where classmates are from) Write about your life (complete a paragraph with personal information)
3. What Interesting Classes!	Comprehension: true-false, questions, matching Vocabulary: antonyms, word identification	Exploring majors while still in ESL	Simple present tense of to be, There is/are, Wh questions	What's in your future? (discussion of talents and careers)
4. How to Study English	Comprehension: true-false, matching phrases Vocabulary: word identification, dictionary words	Study skills and dictionary use	Simple present tense using other verbs	Record homework contacts (asking classmates for phone numbers) Practice a message for your teacher (practicing a phone message) Write a short letter in English (letter to your child's teacher)
5. I Don't Have Time!	Comprehension: sequence, antonyms, scanning words and sentences, inferential questions Vocabulary: words in context	Time and schedule planning for school success	Present tense, third-person singular	Time flies (schedule writing) Where does the day go? (filling in a pie chart) Time to relax (student interviews)
6. An Appointment with the Doctor	Comprehension: sequence, antonyms, scanning words and sentences, inferential questions Vocabulary: antonyms, words in context	Medical office vocabulary	Objective pronouns	Call the doctor! (phone call practice to a doctor) What to do? (brainstorming solutions about unplanned pregnancies)
7. There Are Problems in My House	Comprehension: main idea, scanning words Vocabulary: words in context	Alcohol, drug, and family problems vocabulary	Present progressive	What happens next? (writing a story conclusion) Write and present a dialogue (writing and presenting a dialogue with a partner)
8. Dating and Holidays in the United States	Comprehension: main idea, inferential questions, scanning word lists Vocabulary: words in context	American dating customs and holidays	More practice with objective pronouns	Write a valentine note (paired writing activity) Make that call! (asking someone for a date)

Reading and Skills Chart (continued)

Chapter	Reading Focus	Practical Focus	Grammar Focus	Expansion Activities
9. Looking for a Job	Comprehension: main idea, sequence, scanning for information, inferential questions Vocabulary: words in context	Career and job search vocabulary	Present progressive and simple present tense, third-person singular	Choose a job for Olivia (choose and give reasons) Time for an interview (practice interview skills)
10. What Careers Should I Think About?	Comprehension: graph interpretation, scanning, main idea Vocabulary: words in context, synonyms	Thinking about majors and careers, salary, and education level	*Be + going to +* infinitive for the future	The longer you go to school (interpreting graphs)
11. Personal and Family Counseling	Comprehension: main idea, inferential questions, sequence, scanning paragraphs Vocabulary: words in context, synonyms	Talk to a friend about counseling	Asking and answering questions in the simple past	Create a counseling dialogue (writing and presenting a dialogue)
12. The Community	Comprehension: main idea, inferential questions, sequence, scanning paragraphs Vocabulary: words in context	Community agencies and volunteering	Irregular past tense	Where can I volunteer? (research a community organization)

Introduction

Read to Succeed 1 is the first in a two-part series intended for beginning students. Students learn to read English as they progress through twelve practical and interesting chapters on living in the United States for the first time, college and study skills, culture and survival skills, and jobs, counseling, and community. The text emphasizes communication skills as each chapter presents prereading exercises with photographs or illustrations, readings, comprehension and vocabulary exercises, writing practice, grammar hints, practice reading charts and graphs, and expansion activities. The lessons focus on academic and everyday situations to develop students' vocabulary and their success in oral, listening, reading, and writing skills.

Targeted Level

Read to Succeed 1 was written for beginning students in first-year English as a Second Language reading classes (typically, level 1 in a 3- to 5-level ESL program). Book 1 is geared to students who are literate but who have little or no background in English and for whom learning English is the key to survival and success in school and in U.S. culture in general. Because *Read to Succeed 1* was written with the beginning student in mind, the reading level does not outpace the typical grammar and writing level of a first-semester student. The chapters also follow the grammar and writing sequence commonly found in first-semester ESL texts. The lessons end with comprehensive vocabulary lists, which are also available with definitions and sample sentences in a flashcard format on the Web site http://esl.college.hmco.com/students. *Read to Succeed 2* will target students at the next reading level, high beginning to low intermediate.

Notable Features

Reading Readiness

- ▶ Each chapter begins with prereading exercises that focus students on the content of the reading and include photographs or illustrations. The exercises help students acquire oral language facility and vocabulary in context before reading with the assistance of their teacher.

- ▶ The text gives students an opportunity to improve listening skills. The book's design gives the teacher opportunities to work on improving students' pronunciation through oral reading of words, sentences, and readings.

- ▶ Photographs, illustrations, and charts and graphs make acquisition of vocabulary easy because students can immediately associate images with vocabulary words.

- The vocabulary in the beginning lessons is commonly used words in first-year reading texts. Much of this vocabulary appears again in readings in later chapters.

- Each chapter contains exercises for conversation in a group and in pairs.

Reading Lessons

- Each reading uses carefully controlled syntax, grammar, and verb tenses.

- The **four thematic units** offer readings in the following areas: Our New Country and School; Study Skills and College Success; Survival and Culture; and Careers, Counseling, and Community.

- The **12 chapters** maintain student interest and do not overwhelm the beginning student with grammar structures and vocabulary that are too difficult.

- Chapter 1 includes three short reading selections; Chapters 2–12 have two reading selections each. The first selection can be read by the teacher (if desired) to develop listening skills or by the students aloud in class to work on pronunciation. The second and third reading selections can be used for silent reading. All readings include comprehension exercises with clear directions.

- Each chapter begins with **prereading exercises and questions** that focus students on the content of the reading and include photos or illustrations. The exercises develop student interest before the reading selection. The prereading pages lend themselves to overhead transparencies.

- All chapters include **comprehension, vocabulary, writing, and conversation practice.**

- The **comprehension exercises** include true-false and simple inferential questions, and ask students to identify the main ideas and scan for details.

- **Vocabulary practice** includes matching vocabulary words with definitions; multiple-choice questions; fill-in, scanning, and synonym and antonym exercises; and conversation.

- **Oral practice questions,** which can be used in class in groups and pairs, give students many opportunities to speak in the classroom about a specific topic. The same questions can also be used for written homework.

- **Writing practice** is offered in fill-in, word definition, and complete sentence exercises.

- The units are written in simple, clear, and accessible syntax, enhanced with photographs, illustrations, and charts and graphs.

- The **expansion activities** at the end of each chapter provide follow-up activities to further explore the theme and to provide students with additional opportunities for oral, writing, and vocabulary practice.

▸ The **vocabulary lists,** whether on the Web site http://esl.college.hmco.com/ students or the last page of each chapter, help students review vocabulary, learn the parts of speech, and recognize word families. The Web site list includes definitions.

▸ An **appendix** displays United States and world maps so that students can identify geographical locations mentioned in the text or by the teacher and other students.

▸ Ten of the chapters in *Read to Succeed 1* have been field-tested at Santa Barbara City College in the ESL department's ESL 112 and ESL 116 courses (levels 1 and 2 reading and vocabulary) during the past 14 years. Teachers and students found that the materials were very successful for developing reading and vocabulary skills. We hope you will find them so as well.

▸ An answer key appears on the Web site http://college.hmco.com/esl/ instructors.

ACKNOWLEDGMENTS

We wish to thank:

Joann Kozyrev for initially encouraging us to write this series

Susan Maguire for her dynamic support and approval of this project

Kathy Sands Boehmer for her guidance in the development of this book

Kathleen Smith for her wonderful suggestions and additions

We gratefully acknowledge our reviewers for their valuable input and suggestions:

Anne Bachmann, Clackamas Community College

Anne Bollati, Black Hawk College

Lee Culver, Miami-Dade Community College

Elaine Dow, Quinsigamond Community College

Susan Jamieson, Bellevue Community College

Alan Shute, Bunker Hill Community College

Meena Singhal, Long Beach City College

Garnet Templin-Imel, Bellevue Community College

Special thanks to our families for being so patient while we wrote this book:

Maria Clara Garcia

Cuauhtemoc, Luna, Moctezuma, Quetzal, and Tlaloc Vallejo-Howard

Our New Country and School

Our New Home

Reading 1   Ali's Letter to Mustafa

Before You Read

▶**EXERCISE 1** Discuss these questions with a partner or a small group.

1. Are you a full-time or part-time student?

2. Do you work?

3. Where do you live?

▶**EXERCISE 2** **Listen to your teacher read the sentences. Say the sentences after your teacher. Then match the sentences to the pictures. Write the correct letter next to the sentence.**

A.

B.

C.

D.

E.

F.

G.

H.

1. I study ESL at the community college. ___*A*___

2. These are English sentences. _____

3. She is a hostess at the restaurant. _____

4. We live in an apartment. _____

5. They are excellent students. _____

6. He is a chef at the restaurant. _____

7. It is a Moroccan restaurant. _____

8. They study in high school. _____

▶**EXERCISE 3** **Circle the answer to each question.**

1. What is Denver?   a. A country.   (b. A city.)   c. A state.

2. Parents are   a. Mom and Dad.   b. sisters.   c. all the family.

3. It is snowy   a. at the beach.   b. in the desert.   c. in the mountains.

▶**EXERCISE 4** **Look at the envelope that Ali addressed to Mustafa. Then answer these questions.**

Ali Mansour
145 S. Main Street
Denver, Colorado,
U.S.A. 53662

Mustafa Mansour
53 Blvd. Hassan II
Fez, Morocco

1. What city is Ali in? _____

2. Where is his cousin, Mustafa? _____

3. Where is Morocco? _____

About the picture (circle the correct answer)

4. What is the name of the restaurant?

  a. the French Restaurant

  b. Moroccan Hideaway

  c. Dine In–Take Out

5. The restaurant is

  a. very large.

  b. large.

  c. small.

Words from the Reading*

chef   happy   hostess   parents   similar   snowy

*Your teacher can help you understand these words and others listed at the end of the chapter and on the Web site at http://esl.college.hmco.com/students

Ali is a level-one ESL student. For his homework, he writes a letter in English. Read page 1 of Ali's letter to his cousin, Mustafa.

Page 1

January 21

Dear Cousin Mustafa,

I am in the United States now. How are you? I'm happy. My family is fine.

My **parents** are at the restaurant every day. It is a French restaurant. My father is the chef and manager. My mother is the hostess and **cashier.**

Denver, Colorado, is a nice large city. It's very cold and snowy today. It is hot in summer, and it is cold in winter. Our apartment is large, but it is not **cheap.** The rent is $1,500 per month. We are happy in Denver. Denver is not similar to Fez, but it is nice.

cashier	clerk
cheap	not expensive
parents	mother and father

Comprehension

▶**EXERCISE 5** **Write T (true) or F (false) for each statement. Then discuss your answers with a classmate.**

_____ 1. Ali is in Denver, Colorado.

_____ 2. Mustafa is in Mexico.

_____ 3. Ali's parents work at a Japanese restaurant.

_____ 4. The mother is a cashier and hostess.

_____ 5. Denver is cold in winter.

_____ 6. Denver is a nice city.

_____ 7. The apartment is cheap.

_____ 8. Denver is a small city.

▶**EXERCISE 6** **Write the letter of the phrase that completes or answers the sentence.**

1. Where are Ali's parents every day? _*f*_____

2. Ali's parents work _____

3. Ali's father is a _____

4. Is Ali's mother a hostess? _____

5. What city is the family in? _____

6. Denver is _____

7. They live in _____

8. The apartment is _____

9. They are _____

10. Denver is not _____

a. happy in Denver.

b. an apartment.

c. Denver, Colorado.

d. similar to Fez.

e. Yes, she is a hostess.

f. They are at the restaurant every day.

g. a nice city.

h. large but expensive.

i. at a French restaurant.

j. manager and a chef.

▶**EXERCISE 7** **Answer the questions orally with your teacher. Then answer the questions orally with a classmate. At home, write the answers for homework. Answer in a complete sentence.**

1. Where is Mustafa? _Mustafa is in Fez, Morocco._

2. What city is Ali in? _____

3. What is the name of Mustafa's city? _____

4. Where is Morocco? _____

5. Where are Ali's parents every day? _____

6. What is the father's job? _____

7. What is the mother's job? _____

8. What kind of city is Denver? _____

9. How is the weather in winter? _____

10. Is Ali's apartment cheap? _____

11. How much is the rent? _____

12. Is Denver hot in the summer? _____

Reading 2 Ali's Letter to Mustafa (continued)

Before You Read

▶**EXERCISE 8** **Before you read page 2 of Ali's letter to Mustafa, circle the answer for the following statements. Then read Ali's letter.**

1. The plural of person is   a. persons   (b. people)   c. a person

2. The opposite of near is   a. close   b. next to   c. far

3. A hug is   a. a kiss   b. food   c. an embrace

4. The opposite of friendly is   a. nice   b. friendship   c. unfriendly

5. Different is the opposite of   a. many   b. same   c. differently

6. The plural of American is   a. Americas   b. America   c. Americans

7. The singular of countries is   a. city   b. country   c. counties

▶**EXERCISE 9** **Complete the sentence with a word from the box.**

Mexican	Italy	Morocco	French	English
Arab	Brazil	Japan	Chinese	Spanish

1. The nationality of a person from Mexico is _____ .

2. People in China speak _____ .

3. Where are Brazilians from? _____

4. _____ people speak Arabic.

5. Where do people speak Japanese? _____

6. The nationality of people in France is _____ .

Words from the Reading*

friendly   **full-time**   **nice**   **people**   **well**

*Your teacher can help you understand these words and others listed at the end of the chapter and on the Web site at http://esl.college.hmco.com/students

Page 2

There are 500,000 people in Denver. There are people from different countries here. Americans are very friendly. There is a nice Italian family next door. Every day I say hello to a Mexican family. There are not many Moroccan people here.

My brother and my sister study in high school. Ahmed and Latifah read and write English well. There is a good high school **near** the apartment. My English is not good now.

I also work at the French restaurant at night. I am a waiter. I am not a full-time worker. I work five nights a week. I am always **busy** at my job.

I will write to you again.

A big **hug** from your cousin,
Ali

busy	occupied
hug	embrace
near	close

Comprehension

▶**EXERCISE 10 Read the sentence, then write the letter of the answer.**

1. There are people from __*b*__ in Denver, Colorado.

   a. the same countries   b. different countries   c. Morocco

2. The people in Denver are _____.

   a. not nice   b. unfriendly   c. friendly

3. There _____ many Moroccan families in Denver.

   a. are not   b. are   c. some

4. Latifah and Ahmed study in _____.

   a. middle school   b. high school   c. elementary school

5. Ali's brother and sister read and write English _____.

   a. well   b. badly   c. friendly

Grammar Hints: *There is / there are*

▶**EXERCISE 11 Complete the sentences with the correct form: *there is* or *there are*.**

---

there is (singular): There **is** an Italian **student** (singular) in my class.
there are (plural): There **are** Mexican **students** (plural) also.

---

1. _____*There is*_____ a **boy** from the Ukraine next door.

2. _____ Chinese **people** in my class.

3. _____ a **job** for a waiter in the restaurant.

4. _____ not many **jobs** in my city.

5. _____ many expensive **apartments** in Denver.

► **EXERCISE 12** Complete the sentences with the correct form of *to be*.

Singular	Plural
I **am**	we **are**
you **are**	you **are**
he, she, it **is**	they **are**

1. I _____ from Fez, Morocco.

2. The students _____ in the class.

3. You _____ a good friend.

4. We _____ not French.

5. She _____ my cousin.

6. It _____ difficult to work and study full-time.

Reading Charts and Graphs

▶**EXERCISE 13**

A. Study the immigration graph.

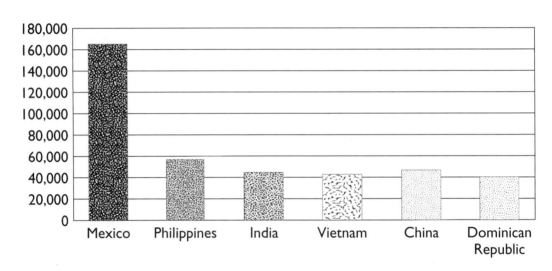

**Legal immigration to the United States
in 1996 from the top six countries**

Source: U.S. Department of Justice, INS, 1996

**B. Answer these questions about the graph. Use *am/is/are* for present tense
and *was/were* for past tense.**

1. Are there numbers and names of countries here? *Yes, there are numbers and names*
   of countries here.

2. What countries are in the graph? _____

   _____

3. Where were the most immigrants from? _____

   _____

4. How many countries are on the graph? _____

   _____

5. Is your country represented in the graph? _____

   _____

Reading 3   Ali's Letter to Mustafa (six months later)

Before You Read

▶**EXERCISE 14** Circle the answer to each question.

1. House is a synonym for   a. neighbor   b. apartment   c. home

2. It is 74°F today. It is   a. warm   b. cold   c. very hot

3. In the summer it is   a. sunny   b. very cold   c. snowy

Words from the Reading*

left   right

*Your teacher can help you understand these words and others listed at the end of the chapter and on the Web site at http://esl.college.hmco.com/students

▶**EXERCISE 15** Scan (read quickly) the reading below and answer these questions.

1. What month is it in the letter? _____

2. How is Ali's English now? (the same or more advanced?) _____

   _____

3. How many paragraphs are there? _____

Read another letter that Ali writes to his cousin, Mustafa, six months later.

June 22

Dear Cousin Mustafa,

How are you? I hope my uncle, my aunt, and you are well. My family and I are well, **also.** Today it is warm and **sunny** in Denver because it is **summer.**

My classes and my new home are very interesting. I study English as a Second Language (ESL) at the community college. It is not a large college, but it is a very good school. I study hard every day. English is difficult, and it is different from **Arabic.** I read from left to right. The alphabet and letters are different. There are **capital letters** and small letters. I write paragraphs now with many sentences.

My new classmates are excellent students. The English teachers here are friendly. There are nice ESL students from many countries in my classes. I speak English with my classmates, and now I also speak English with Americans. I practice English every day.

With love from your cousin,
Ali

also	too
Arabic	Middle Eastern language
capital letter	large letter
summer	the hot time of the year
sunny	a lot of sun

Comprehension

▶**EXERCISE 16** Read the questions and answer them orally with your teacher. Then answer the questions orally with a classmate. At home, write the answers for homework. Answer in complete sentences.

1. Is Ali a student at the community college?

   <u>*Yes, he is a student at the community college.*</u> Or _____<u>*Yes, he is.*</u>_____

                      long answer   short answer

2. Is he an ESL student? _____

   _____

3. Is English easy or difficult? _____

   _____

4. Is English different from Arabic? _____

   _____

5. Is English interesting or boring? _____

   _____

6. Are English letters different for Ali? _____

   _____

7. Are the English teachers unfriendly? _____

   _____

8. Are there excellent students in Ali's classes? _____

   _____

Vocabulary Practice

▶**EXERCISE 17** Help Ali write another letter to Mustafa. Write the correct word from the box to complete each sentence.

| cultures | friends | ~~happy~~ | life | new | people | restaurants | together |

I am _____*happy*_____ in the United States, but everything is different. The food, music, language, schools, and customs are _____. My _____ is very interesting. There are many American _____ in my neighborhood. We can try different kinds of food. There are many American, Italian, Chinese, Japanese, and Mexican _____. There is also a good Moroccan restaurant in Denver. My new _____ at school and work are from Brazil, Mexico, Japan, Haiti, China, and Sweden. We all work and study _____. The different _____, languages, and people are nice.

▶**EXERCISE 18** Write the correct *adjective* from the box to complete each sentence.

| ~~different~~ | friendly | good | happy | interesting | young |

1. There are people with _____*different*_____ cultures and customs here.

2. My neighbors are very _____ people. They always say "Hello."

3. There are _____ and old people at school.

4. My new life is very _____ because there are many cultures here.

5. My family and I are _____ in Denver.

6. There are _____ and bad restaurants here.

▶**EXERCISE 19** **Write the correct antonym for the <u>underlined</u> words. (An antonym is a word with the opposite meaning.) Read Ali's letters on pages 5, 9, and 14 again if necessary.**

different	excited	expensive	friendly	full-time	good	happy
hot	interesting	large	many	~~tall~~	together	

1. I am <u>short</u>. I am not _____*tall*_____.

2. The college is not <u>small</u>. It is _____.

3. My neighbors are not <u>unfriendly</u>. They are _____.

4. Our apartment is not <u>cheap</u>. It is _____.

5. There are <u>few</u> Moroccans here, but there are _____ Americans.

6. We are not <u>unhappy</u> in Denver. We are _____ here.

7. I do not work <u>part-time</u>. I work _____.

8. Denver is not a <u>bad</u> city. It is a _____ city.

9. My life is not <u>boring</u>. It is _____ because there are different cultures.

10. The cultures here are not the <u>same</u>. They are _____.

11. I am not <u>bored</u> in the United States. I am _____ about my new life.

12. My friends and I do not study <u>separately</u>. We study _____ at school.

13. It is summer now, and the weather isn't <u>cold</u>. It's _____ and sunny.

Expansion Activities

▶ **Activity 1 Make a Family Tree** *A family tree is a chart of a family—parents, aunts, uncles, grandparents, cousins, brothers and sisters, and sons and daughters—that shows how the family members are related to each other. Here is an example of a family tree:*

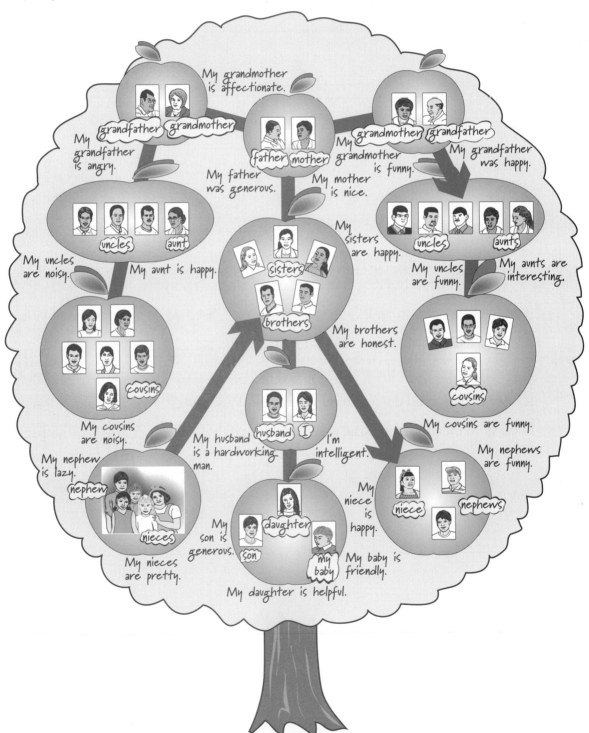

A. Draw your family tree. Draw each person's face or use photos. Label each person with his or her name and relationship to you.

B. Then write sentences about five people in your family tree. Use an adjective and a form of the verb "to be" in each sentence.

My mother is an intelligent woman.

Use the vocabulary in the box to help you.

Family

grandfather	grandmother	father	mother	daughter	son
aunt	uncle	nephew	niece	cousin	
parents	husband	wife	brother	sister	

Adjectives

artistic	energetic	friendly	funny	generous
hardworking	honest	intelligent	kind	loud
patient	quiet	responsible	serious	studious

C. Share your family tree with your classmates. Read your sentences and show your family tree to a classmate. Then ask questions about your classmate's family tree.

▶ Activity 2   Write a Letter to Your Classmate

A. Ask a classmate these questions. Write the answers.

1. What is your first name? _____

2. What is your last name? _____

3. What is your street address? _____

4. What city and state do you live in? _____

5. What is your zip code? _____

B. Write your name, address, city, state, and zip code on the envelope. Also write your classmate's name, address, city, state, and zip code on the envelope. If you need help, look back at Ali's envelope on page 4.

C. Use this form to help you write a letter to your classmate.

_____
(Date)

Dear _____,
(Name of your classmate)

_____

_____

_____

_____

_____

_____

_____,

_____
(Your Name)

Vocabulary List

Adjectives

all

artistic

bored / excited[1]

boring / interesting

busy

cheap / expensive

cold / hot

cold / warm

different / same

difficult / easy

energetic

excellent / terrible

few / many

fine

five

friendly / unfriendly

full-time / part-time

funny

generous

good

happy / unhappy

hardworking

honest

intelligent

kind

large / small

left

loud

my

new

nice

one

patient

quiet

responsible

right

serious

short / tall

similar

snowy

some

studious

sunny

young

Nationalities[2]

American

Brazilian

Chinese

French

Haitian

Italian

Japanese

Mexican

Moroccan

Swedish

Adverbs

also

badly

now

today

together / separately

very

well

Nouns

apartment

Arabic

beach / beaches

boy

city / cities

college

country / countries

culture

custom

desert

elementary school

embrace

English

food

friend

high school

home

hug

January

job

kiss / kisses

language

life / lives

middle school

month

mountain

music

neighbor

neighborhood

next door

night

people

person

rent

restaurant

state

student

summer

winter

Family

aunt

brother

cousin

Dad

daughter

father

grandfather

grandmother

husband

Mom

mother

nephew

niece

parents

sister

son

uncle

wife

Jobs

cashier

chef

hostess

manager

teacher

waiter

Prepositions

close to

far from

near

next to

1. Paired adjectives and adverbs are antonyms (opposites).
2. Nationalities can be adjectives or nouns.

Subject Pronouns	you (plural)	is	**Expressions**	antonym
I	they	live	There is	capital letter
you (singular)	**Verbs**	study	There are	paragraph
he	am	to be		read
she	are	work	**Reading Words** [3]	sentence
it	hope	write	adjective	small letter
we	speak		alphabet	

3. These are some other words to help you with your reading work.

 If you want to review vocabulary and complete additional activities related to this unit, go to the Read to Succeed 1 Web site at http://esl.college.hmco.com/students

CHAPTER 2
Life in the United States

Reading 1   Immigrants in the United States

Before You Read

▶**EXERCISE 1** Discuss these questions with a partner or a small group.

1. Where are you from?

2. What is your nationality?

3. What is your native language?

▶**EXERCISE 2** **Listen to your teacher read the sentences. Say the sentences after your teacher. Then match the sentences to the pictures. Write the correct letter next to the sentence.**

A. Gloria is from Haiti. **B. Juan is from Mexico.** **C. Xi is from China.** **D. Vasyl is from the Ukraine.**

What is their nationality?

1. Gloria is Haitian. ___*A*___

2. Vasyl's nationality is Ukrainian. _____

3. Juan's nationality is Mexican. _____

4. Xi is Chinese. _____

E. She is a doctor. **F. He is a nurse.** **G. She is a cashier.** **H. He is an auto mechanic.**

What is their job?

5. He is at the garage. _____

6. She is at the hospital. _____

7. She is at the supermarket. _____

8. He is at the clinic. _____

▶**EXERCISE 3** For each word, write an *X* in the correct category. Some words are in two categories.

	Nationality	Country	Language
Chinese			
Dominican Republic		*X*	
Mexican			
Ukrainian			
Vietnam			

Words from the Reading*

ask   hardworking   immigrant   nationality

*Your teacher can help you understand these words and others listed at the end of the chapter and on the Web site at http://esl.college.hmco.com/students

▶**EXERCISE 4** Scan (read quickly) the reading for the answers to these questions.

1. What is the title of the reading? *"Immigrants in the United States"*

2. What is an immigrant? _____

   _____

3. What are some nationalities of immigrants in the United States? _____

   _____

4. The main idea (the most important idea) of this reading is underlined in the first paragraph. Write it here: _____

   _____

Read a school newspaper story about two immigrants, Anh and José.

Immigrants in the United States

There are many immigrants in the United States. There are people from many different **countries** and nationalities in the English as a Second Language (ESL) classroom. There are students from the Dominican Republic, Mexico, Vietnam, Guatemala, and the Ukraine. There are also Salvadorans, Chinese, and Laotian students. Anh Chang and José García are hardworking students in the ESL program. Anh is from the People's Republic of China, and José is from Mexico.

Anh and José learn about the differences in the many **cultures** of the people at work and the students in their classroom. The students speak a variety of languages, and their customs are different, too. José and Anh talk about these differences. They ask their classmates about their life experiences, their education in their native country, their families, work, **travel,** and **hobbies.** José and Anh also see many **similarities** among the students.

country	nation
culture	set of traditions
hobby	free-time activities
similarity	shared quality
travel	journey to a different place

Comprehension

▶**EXERCISE 5** **Write T (true) or F (false) for each statement. Then discuss your answers with a classmate.**

__T__ 1. There are many immigrants in the United States.

_____ 2. There are students from different countries here.

_____ 3. There are only two nationalities in the United States.

_____ 4. Anh and José are not hardworking.

_____ 5. Anh is Chinese, and José is Mexican.

_____ 6. Mexico, Vietnam, and Guatemala are countries.

▶**EXERCISE 6** Answer the *wh + be* questions orally with your teacher. Then answer the questions orally with a classmate. At home, write the answers for homework. Answer in complete sentences.

***Wh* questions:**

Where   about a place   **Who**   about a person   **What**   about a thing

---

1. What is the title of the reading? _The title of the reading is "Immigrants in the_ _United States."_

2. Where is Anh Chang from? _____

   _____

3. Who is Mexican? _____

   _____

4. In Anh and José's class, are there students with different customs and languages?

   _____

   _____

5. Anh and José ask their classmates about their life experiences. What are some of those life experiences? _____

   _____

▶**EXERCISE 7** In class, practice interviewing another student. At home, answer the questions about you.

1. What is your name? _____

   _____

2. What is your nationality? _____

   _____

3. Are you hardworking? _____

   _____

4. Who is your reading teacher? _____

_____

5. What is your job? *My job is . . . . I am a . . . .* _____

_____

6. Where is your teacher from? *My teacher is from . . . . Our teacher is from . . . .*

_____

_____

7. Are there students from different countries in your class? *Yes, there are students from different countries in my (our) class.*

8. Where is your family? _____

_____

9. What are your hobbies? _____

_____

10. Are there similarities among the students in your class? _____

_____

_____

11. From what countries are the students in your class? _____

_____

12. What languages do the students in your class speak? _____

_____

13. What language do people use in your native country? _____

_____

Vocabulary Practice

▶**EXERCISE 8** **Read the sentence, then write the letter of the answer.**

1. Salvadoran, Vietnamese, and Cuban are ___*b*___.
   a. countries   b. nationalities   c. days

2. Anh is from _____.
   a. Iran   b. Cambodia   c. the People's Republic of China

3. José's nationality is _____.
   a. Guatemalan   b. Japanese   c. Mexican

4. Anh and José are from _____ countries.
   a. different   b. the same   c. three

5. There are ESL students from a _____ of countries.
   a. variety   b. customs   c. similarity

6. People _____ to different countries to visit interesting new places.
   a. work   b. travel   c. write

7. I _____ a new student in the classroom.
   a. hobbies   b. work   c. see

8. Anh and her sister _____ Chinese.
   a. speak   b. family   c. ask

▶**EXERCISE 9** **Write the correct adjective of nationality from the box to complete each sentence.**

~~American~~	British (English)	Chinese	Cuban	French
Iranian	Japanese	Korean	Moroccan	Spanish

1. Maria is from the United States. She is _____*American*_____.

2. Mr. Kim is from Seoul, Korea. He is _____.

3. Horoko's nationality is _____. She is from Tokyo, Japan.

4. Rania is from Tangier, Morocco, and her nationality is _____.

5. Juan is from Havana, Cuba. He is _____.

6. Sharon is from London, England. Her nationality is _____.

7. Farideh's nationality is _____. She is from Tehran, Iran.

8. Anh is from Shanghai, China. Her nationality is _____.

9. Manolo is from Malaga, Spain. His nationality is _____.

10. Sylvie's native country is France. She is _____.

Reading 2 "A New Life"

Before You Read

▶**EXERCISE 10** **For each word, write an** *X* **in the correct category.**

	Jobs	Places People Work
attendant	*X*	
butcher		
cashier		
gas station		
market		
waitress		

▶**EXERCISE 11** **Scan (read quickly) the reading for the answers to these questions.**

1. What is the title? _____

2. What are Anh and José's jobs? _____

_____

3. Is life in the United States easy or difficult for them? _____

_____

4. The main idea (the most important idea) of each paragraph is <u>underlined</u>. Write the main idea of the first paragraph here. _____

_____

Read a story about Anh and José in *The Independent,* a community newspaper.

"A New Life"

Life in the United States is interesting but difficult for Anh and José. Anh and José are full-time workers. Anh is a cashier during the day at the Indo-Chinese Market. José is an attendant at a gasoline station at night. Their jobs are interesting. They practice English every day, but the pay is not good. It is $5.75 per hour. Anh and José's pay is low, and **expenses** are very high in the United States. They do not speak English well, and some customers are impatient with them. Life is difficult for Anh and José because they work and study many hours.

Anh and José have some difficulties, but they are also happy. Anh is married, and her husband is a **butcher** at the market. José is **single,** and his favorite customer is Jackie, a nice American girl. She is a **waitress** at a restaurant. Anh and José know there are many opportunities for **bilingual** people in the United States. Life is interesting because they study and work, and there are many cultures here.

In class, Anh and José talk about life in the United States. They ask, "Life in the United States is difficult and also interesting now, but what is our future in the United States?"

bilingual	two languages
butcher	meat cutter
expense	something you pay for
single	not married
waitress	woman waiter at a restaurant (also waitperson)

 **Comprehension**

▶**EXERCISE 12** **Write the letter of the phrase that completes each sentence.**

1. Anh and José are _____
2. Anh is a cashier _____
3. José is an attendant _____
4. Their jobs are interesting _____
5. Anh and José _____
6. Anh's husband is _____
7. José's favorite customer is ___*b*___
8. Life in the United States is difficult _____

a. but the pay is not good.

b. an American girl.

c. for José and Anh.

d. at a gasoline station.

e. at the Indo-Chinese market.

f. a butcher at the market.

g. full-time workers.

h. practice English every day.

 Vocabulary Practice

▶**EXERCISE 13** **Write an antonym for each word. (An antonym is a word with the opposite meaning.)**

1. at night _____
2. patient _____
3. bad _____

4. single _____
5. easy _____
6. unhappy _____

►**EXERCISE 14 Say these occupation words, then write the name of the job under the picture:**

businesswoman	butcher	carpenter	cashier
computer programmer	doctor	farmworker	gas station attendant
~~police officer~~	waitress	TV announcer	

A. _police_
      officer

B. _____

C. _____

D. _____

E. _____

F. _____

G. _____

H. _____

I. _____

J. _____

K. _____

►**EXERCISE 15** **Complete each sentence with a word from the box.**

A. Adjectives

bilingual	different	many	hardworking	married

1. Lanh speaks Vietnamese and English, so she is _____*bilingual*_____.

2. The students in this class all are from _____ cultures.

3. José studies very hard. He is a _____ student.

4. Andre is _____. His wife is very nice.

5. I need more money so I want a _____ job.

B. Nouns

customer	expenses	market	pay	title

1. Yui works in a _____. She is a cashier.

2. The _____ wants to buy some apples.

3. "Read to Succeed" is the _____ of this book.

4. He has many _____ but very low pay.

5. I want a job with good _____.

C. Names of Jobs

carpenter	doctor	police officer	programmer	waiter

1. John works in a restaurant. He is a _____.

2. Maria is a good _____. Many people visit her when they are sick.

3. A _____ has a dangerous job.

4. I want to be a _____. I like to make things.

5. A computer _____ makes a lot of money.

Grammar Hints: Possessive Adjectives

▶**EXERCISE 16** Complete the sentences with the correct possessive adjective.

Subject Pronouns	Possessive Adjectives
I	my
you	your
he, she, it	his, her, its
we	our
they	their

1. He writes on _____*his*_____ paper.

2. You love _____ children.

3. She helps _____ friends.

4. We talk to _____ classmates.

5. I want _____ CD back, please.

Expansion Activities

▶ **Activity 1   Use a Map**   *With your teacher, mark a map to show where people in your class are from. Then write sentences about the nationalities of the people in your class.*

Examples:

Hae Kae is from Korea. He speaks Korean.

Gloria is from Costa Rica. She is Costa Rican.

▶**Activity 2   Write about Your Life** *Complete these sentences about your life in the United States.*

My name is _____. I am a _____*full-time*_____ (full-time/part-time)

worker. I am a _____ (job) at _____ (day/night) at

a _____ (place where you work). My job is _____

(interesting/difficult/easy). The pay is _____ (good/bad). I am

_____ (single/married). I am studying _____

(classes you take) at _____ (name of your school). My life is

_____ (easy/difficult/happy).

Vocabulary List

Adjectives

bad

bilingual

impatient

low

married

patient

serious

single

three

Possessive Adjectives

her

his

its

my

our

their

your

Nationalities

British (English)

Cuban

Guatemalan

Iranian

Korean

Salvadoran

Spanish

Ukrainian

Vietnamese

Adverbs

here

where

Nouns

classroom

computer

customer

day

difficulty / difficulties

expense

family

future

gas station

hobby / hobbies

immigrant

market

name

nationality / nationalities

night

opportunity / opportunities

pay

program

similarity / similarities

travel

variety / varieties

Countries

Cambodia

Guatemala

Iran

Korea

Mexico

People's Republic of China (or China)

United States

Vietnam

Jobs

announcer

attendant

businesswoman

butcher

carpenter

doctor

farmworker

mechanic

police officer

programmer

waitress

Pronouns

what

who

Verbs

ask

see

speak

travel

Reading Words*

answer

listen

match

say

sentence

title

*These are some other words to help you with your reading work.

If you want to review vocabulary and complete additional activities related to this unit, go to the Read to Succeed 1 Web site at http://esl.college.hmco.com/students

2

Study Skills and College Success

COLLEGE

Time

Study Skills

CAREER

Interests

Planning

ENGLISH

CHAPTER 3

What Interesting Classes!

Reading 1   Colleges and Degrees in the United States

Before You Read

▶**EXERCISE 1** Discuss these questions with a partner or a small group.

1. Which career in the pictures is the most interesting to you?

2. Where do these people work?

3. Do students study for these careers at your school?

4. What other careers are interesting to you?

▶EXERCISE 2 Match the sentence with the picture: What fields do these people work in?

A. business administration

B. photography

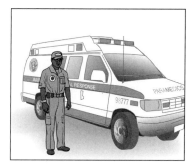

C. emergency medicine

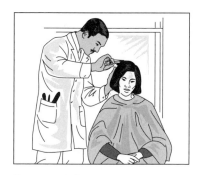

D. cosmetology

E. hotel and restaurant management

F. auto mechanics

1. He is a paramedic. _____

2. He takes pictures of interesting people. _____

3. She is vice president of a company. _____

4. He is the chef at the restaurant. _____

5. He works full-time at the garage. _____

6. He cuts hair part-time at the beauty shop. _____

▶EXERCISE 3 Write T (true) or F (false) for each statement.

_____ 1. A degree is similar to a certificate.

_____ 2. Counseling and mechanics are similar.

_____ 3. "Transfer" is similar to "move or change."

▶**EXERCISE 4** **Answer these questions.**

1. What kinds of college degrees are there? _____

   _____

2. What are the age, sex, and ethnicity of students at a city college? _____

   _____

3. What student services are there at a city college? _____

   _____

4. What classes are there for ESL students? _____

   _____

5. The main idea (the most important idea) of each paragraph below is <u>underlined</u>.
   What is the main idea of the first paragraph? Write it here. _____

   _____

Words from the Reading*

counseling   **mathematics**   **mechanics**   **practical**

*Your teacher can help you understand these words and others listed at the end
of the chapter and on the Web site at http://esl.college.hmco.com/students

---

Read about kinds of colleges in the United States.

⌒ Colleges and Degrees in the United States

There are different kinds of colleges and **degrees** in the United States. A community or city college is for students who are eighteen years old or high school graduates. Community college students sometimes **transfer,** or change, to a university after two years. Some students study at a state college or university for two to four years. A student receives a certificate or an associate **degree** at a community college after two years. At a university, a student can receive a bachelor's **degree** after four years, a master's **degree** after two years, or a doctorate after five to seven years.

There are many city colleges in the United States and they offer many programs and services. Another name for a city college is a community college. City colleges are excellent schools. Students complete the first two years of college classes. City colleges are not expensive, and the classes are very practical and interesting. There are both young and old students at a city college. Single and married students also enroll in classes. There are American students and students from other countries. Students study full-time or part-time during the day or at night. City colleges provide many services for students. There is a financial aid office, a library, a bookstore, a cafeteria, an admissions office, a **counseling** office, a career center, and a nurse's office.

For students from another country, there are English as a Second Language (ESL) classes in grammar, writing, reading, and conversation. Some students take classes in art, mathematics, and auto mechanics while they study ESL. After ESL classes, city colleges offer many other exciting classes and programs.

counseling	giving helpful school information
degree	a college diploma
transfer	move to another program or school

Comprehension

▶**EXERCISE 5** Write T (true) or F (false) for each statement.

_____ 1. A community college is for young children.

_____ 2. There are different degrees at a city college.

_____ 3. Only American students study at a city college.

_____ 4. City colleges do not offer associate degrees.

_____ 5. There are no services at a city college.

_____ 6. There are no ESL classes for students at a city college.

_____ 7. All ESL students study mechanics.

_____ 8. Some ESL students take other classes.

_____ 9. Some students transfer to a university after two years at a city college.

_____ 10. No students receive an associate degree or certificate after two years at a city college.

▶**EXERCISE 6** **Read the questions and answer them orally with your teacher. Then answer the questions orally with a classmate. At home, write the answers for homework. Answer in complete sentences.**

There is (singular)	**There are** (plural)
Is there **a library** at the college?	**Are** there many **students**?
Yes, there **is** a library.	Yes, there **are** many students.

1. Are there city colleges in your state? _____

_____

2. Is there a financial aid office at your college? _____

_____

3. Are ESL classes for English speakers? _____

_____

4. Are city colleges for adults? _____

_____

5. What classes are there in ESL? _____

_____

6. What is another name for a city college? _____

_____

7. What degrees are there in college? _____

_____

8. Is there a nurse's office at a city college? _____

_____

9. Are there students from different countries? _____

_____

10. What classes are there after ESL classes? _____

_____

📖 Vocabulary Practice

▶**EXERCISE 7** **Circle the answer that completes each sentence.**

1. Some community colleges offer an associate _____.
    a. certificate   b. degree   c. diploma

2. Another name for a city college is a _____ college.
    a. community   b. doctorate   c. excellent

3. City colleges are _____.
    a. boring   b. exciting   c. practical

4. There are ESL classes for _____ students.
    a. all   b. American   c. immigrant or visiting

5. You can study the first two years of _____ at a city college.
    a. college classes   b. junior high   c. primary school

6. Students are very happy to receive a _____ after they finish college.
    a. complete   b. degree   c. practical

▶**EXERCISE 8** **Write an antonym from the box for each <u>underlined</u> word. (An antonym is a word with the opposite meaning.)**

cheap	different	easy	
many	night	old	single

1. There are five <u>married</u> women in class. _____

2. That book is very <u>expensive</u>. _____

3. There are many <u>young</u> students in my grammar class. _____

4. There are a <u>few</u> students from Japan in my class. _____

5. My wife and I are <u>day</u> students. _____

6. This test is very <u>difficult</u> for me. _____

7. My teachers are from the <u>same</u> country. _____

Reading Charts and Graphs

▶EXERCISE 9

A. Study the information in the graph about education and salary.

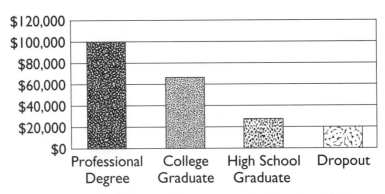

How much money do people make per year?

Professional degree (doctors, lawyers, veterinarians, dentists): $99,300; college graduates (bachelor of arts degree): $45,400; high school graduates: $25,900; high school dropouts: $18,900

Source: U.S. Census, 1999

B. Answer these questions about the bar graph.

1. What is the salary for a high school dropout? _____

2. Who earns more money, a college graduate or a high school graduate?

   _____

3. Who makes almost $100,000 per year? _____

4. Does a person make more money if she or he studies more? _____

Reading 2   After ESL

Before You Read

▶**EXERCISE 10** **Discuss these questions with a partner or a small group.**

1. A major is an area of study, and a career is a profession. True or false?

2. Chemistry is a science. True or false?

3. There are no numbers used in accounting. True or false?

4. Are there any short programs of study after ESL?

5. What are some possible programs of study?

6. What are some ways to decide on your major?

7. What certificate or degree program is interesting for you?

8. What careers in your native country are interesting for you?

9. City colleges are very expensive. True or false?

10. Are there computer classes at your college?

11. What classes are there after the ESL Program?

12. The main idea (the most important idea) of each paragraph in the following reading is <u>underlined</u>. What is the main idea of the second paragraph? Write it here:

_____

_____

_____

Words from the Reading*

business   **chef**   **engineering**   **health care**

*Your teacher can help you understand these words and others listed at the end of
the chapter and on the Web site at http://esl.college.hmco.com/students

---

Read about majors and careers after ESL.

After ESL

<u>What is in your future?</u> An exciting **career** in computers? Engineering? Business? Health care? What are you interested in? Maybe you already have plans for a **career,** or maybe you want to see what **careers** there are. You want to learn English now, but it is important to know about future possibilities.

<u>After ESL, there are many opportunities to study for many **careers.**</u> Some programs require only a short amount of time for the student to receive a certificate. In some colleges, for example, there are one-semester programs in secretarial sciences or the use of computers. At other community colleges, auto mechanics, drafting, and cosmetology are one-year programs. Students study for a certificate or a two-year degree. Some students **enroll** in a two-year degree or certificate program to study business or hotel and restaurant management. Other students study for two years and then transfer to a four-year college or university to study languages, teaching, biology, computer science, mathematics, music, and other **majors.** After two years, some students graduate and then work in their new careers. Some continue to study while they work.

<u>What is a good area for you to study?</u> Maybe you have special interests and talents. For example, people who like to cook study for a **career** as a chef. People who enjoy working with numbers study for a degree in business or accounting. Talk to other students and your teachers to get more ideas. Look for information in the admissions or advising office to see what programs your college offers. There are many possibilities for you after ESL classes.

career	occupation
enroll	register and take classes
major	area of study in college

Comprehension

►**EXERCISE 11** **Write the letter of the correct answer.**

1. What is in the future for an ESL student? _____
2. Are there short programs after ESL? _____
3. What is an example of a one-year program? _____
4. What do some students do after they study for two years? _____
5. Are there services at a college to help students choose a career? _____

a. Cosmetology.

b. They transfer to a four-year college or university.

c. Yes, there is information in the admissions or counseling office.

d. There are many possibilities in the future.

e. Yes, there are short programs.

Vocabulary Practice

►**EXERCISE 12** **Complete each sentence with a word from the box.**

auto mechanics	biology	cosmetology	ESL
hotel and restaurant management	mathematics	music	nursing
photography	secretarial		

1. Juan studies grammar and reading, and he goes to the language lab. He is in the _____ program at City College.

2. Mr. Perez is next to the car in the garage. He is in the _____ program.

3. Maria works in the cafeteria from 8:00–4:00. She is in the _____ program.

4. The students at the beauty college are in the _____ program.

5. I am in the biological science lab. I study in the _____ program.

6. Kim studies calculus and algebra in the _____ department.

7. They are developing photos in the photo lab. They study _____ with Ms. Jones.

8. Ana is in the keyboarding lab in the _____ department.

9. The classes in the _____ program are at the hospital or clinic.

10. She studies piano and guitar in the _____ department.

▶**EXERCISE 13** **Write the letter of the word or words in column 2 that goes with the places in column 1.**

1. admissions office _____   a. application

2. bookstore _____   b. borrow books (free)

3. cafeteria ___*d*_____   c. buy books ($$)

4. cashier's office _____   d. a complete lunch

5. computer lab _____   e. help with ESL classes

6. ESL office _____   f. help with moncy

7. financial aid office _____   g. keyboarding program

8. library _____   h. medical help

9. nurse's office _____   i. pay for classes

10. snack shop _____   j. snacks

▶**EXERCISE 14** **Answer each question with a complete sentence, using the words in the box.**

chef or cook	mechanic	musician
photographer	police officer	teacher

1. Mr. Sanchez teaches at City College. What is his job? _____

   _____

2. Maria works for the police department. What is her career? _____

   _____

3. She takes her car to the garage two times a year. Who repairs her car? _____

   _____

4. Sam plays the saxophone in a jazz band. What is his profession? _____

   _____

5. Joe takes photographs for the newspaper. What is his profession? _____

_____

6. My brother works in an elegant restaurant. What is his job? _____

_____

▶**EXERCISE 15** **Write the job or career next to the major (see the vocabulary list at the end of the chapter).**

Major	**Career**
1. automotive services	*mechanic* _____
2. business administration	_____
3. cosmetology	_____
4. education	_____
5. engineering	_____
6. photography	_____

▶**EXERCISE 16** **Complete each sentence with a word from the box.**

bad	cheap	enroll	few	hardworking	large	many	young

1. There are _____ nationalities in the ESL classes.

2. My professor is twenty-one years old. He is very _____.

3. It is _____ to drop out of high school.

4. This used textbook is $2.00. It is very _____.

5. There are many _____ students in my classes. They do a lot of work.

6. There are 20,000 students at the university. It is a _____ school.

7. There are only two students from France in my class. There are _____ French students in my class.

8. I need to register for my classes. I want to _____ in my classes for next semester.

▶**EXERCISE 17** **Write the word that is the opposite (antonym) of the underlined word.**

1. The books in the bookstore are <u>cheap</u>. _____

2. My friend is a <u>day</u> student. _____

3. My sister is not <u>married</u>. _____

4. My English classes are <u>difficult</u>. _____

5. That is a <u>boring</u> movie. _____

▶**EXERCISE 18** **Study the parts of a book. Then answer the questions in complete sentences.**

1. Title
2. Author

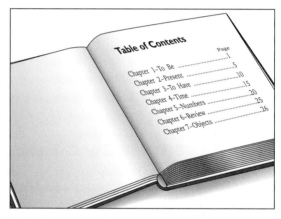

3. Table of contents

4. Chapter title

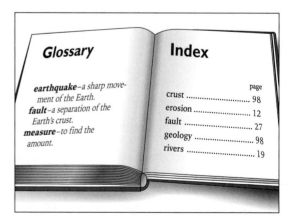

5. Glossary   6. Index

1. What is the title of the book? _____

   _____

2. Who is Rosa Chang? _____

   _____

3. What is in the table of contents? _____

   _____

4. Why is the chapter title important? _____

   _____

5. Where are the definitions? _____

   _____

6. Where is the list of subjects in the book? _____

   _____

Expansion Activity

►**Activity   What's in Your Future?**   *Answer these questions, then talk about your answers with a classmate and your teacher.*

1. What are your special talents or interests? _____

   _____

2. What careers are there for these talents or interests? _____

   _____

3. What information about careers is there in the admissions or advising office of your college? _____

   _____

Vocabulary List

Adjectives

advising

complete

dumb / intelligent

exciting

old / young

other

practical

visiting

Conjunction

while

Nouns

admissions office

beauty shop

bookstore

business / businesses

cafeteria

career

career center

certificate

city college

class / classes

community college

company / companies

composition

computer lab

counseling office

dance

degree

diploma

ESL

executive

financial aid

graduation

grammar

hair

junior high

lab

library / libraries

major

nurse

office

piano

picture

primary school

reading

school

science

service

snack shop

trumpet

university / universities

vice president

ways

writing

Careers / Jobs

art / artist

biology / biologist

business / businessman, businesswoman, businessperson

chemistry / chemist

cosmetology / cosmetologist

counseling / counselor

drafting / draftsman

drama / actress or actor

engineering / engineer

geography / geographer

health care / health care professional

hotel and restaurant management / manager

languages / linguist

mathematics / mathematician

music / musician

nursing / nurse

photography / photographer

physical education / coach

secretarial / secretary

teaching / teacher

word processing / keyboarder

College Degrees

associate in arts (2 years)

associate in science (2 years)

bachelor of arts (4 years)

bachelor of science (4 years)

master of arts (2 years)

master of science (2 years)

doctorate (5–7 years)

Prepositions

after

next to

Verbs

complete

cut

drop out

enroll

graduate

like

offer

provide

receive

take

 If you want to review vocabulary and complete additional activities related to this unit, go to the Read to Succeed 1 Web site at http://esl.college.hmco.com/students

CHAPTER 4

How to Study English

Reading 1 How to Study and Learn English

Before You Read

▶**EXERCISE 1** What is important at school? Write the letter of the picture that matches the answer.

A. **B.** **C.**

1. Be serious and study. _____

2. Take your school materials to class. _____

3. Ask questions in class. _____

4. What else is important at school? Write your ideas here: _____

_____

_____

▶**EXERCISE 2** When is English important? Write the letter of the picture that matches the answer.

A. **B.** **C.**

1. We need English for speaking on the phone. _____

2. We often have to write letters in English. _____

3. English is useful with the doctor. _____

4. When else is English important? Write your ideas here: _____

_____

_____

►**EXERCISE 3** **Draw a line from each word to the picture it matches.**

eraser   three-ring binder   medicine

►**EXERCISE 4** **Answer the questions.**

1. Why is English important? _____

_____

_____

2. What are some good ways to learn English? _____

_____

_____

3. What materials are important for class? _____

_____

_____

4. The main idea (the most important idea) of each paragraph below is <u>underlined</u>. What is the main idea of the third paragraph? Write it here: _____

_____

Read some useful information about school.

How to Study and Learn English

English is important for new immigrants in the United States. Why is English necessary here? English is **useful** at work, home, and school for many reasons: to talk on the phone, to keep a job, to talk to a doctor, to ask for medicine, to write a letter, to get immigration papers, or to communicate during an emergency.

People study languages in different ways. Some people use English on the street or at their job. Some people listen to the radio or television. Some people prefer listening to music; others enjoy learning English by watching cartoons, the news, or other TV programs. Books and newspapers are one way to learn a lot of English vocabulary. Another way is to take English classes at school.

Excellent students are **serious** about school. They are in class on time every day. When they are absent, they call another student or the teacher about the work they missed. They study and take their materials to class. They use a **three-ring binder,** paper, pencils, erasers, pens, and a dictionary. They listen to the teachers and ask questions in class. When they have a problem, good students talk to the teacher or make an appointment with a tutor. When there is a test, they study the night before. Hardworking students study at home daily. For homework, they use a pen and $8\frac{1}{2}'' \times 11''$ paper. The homework papers often look like this:

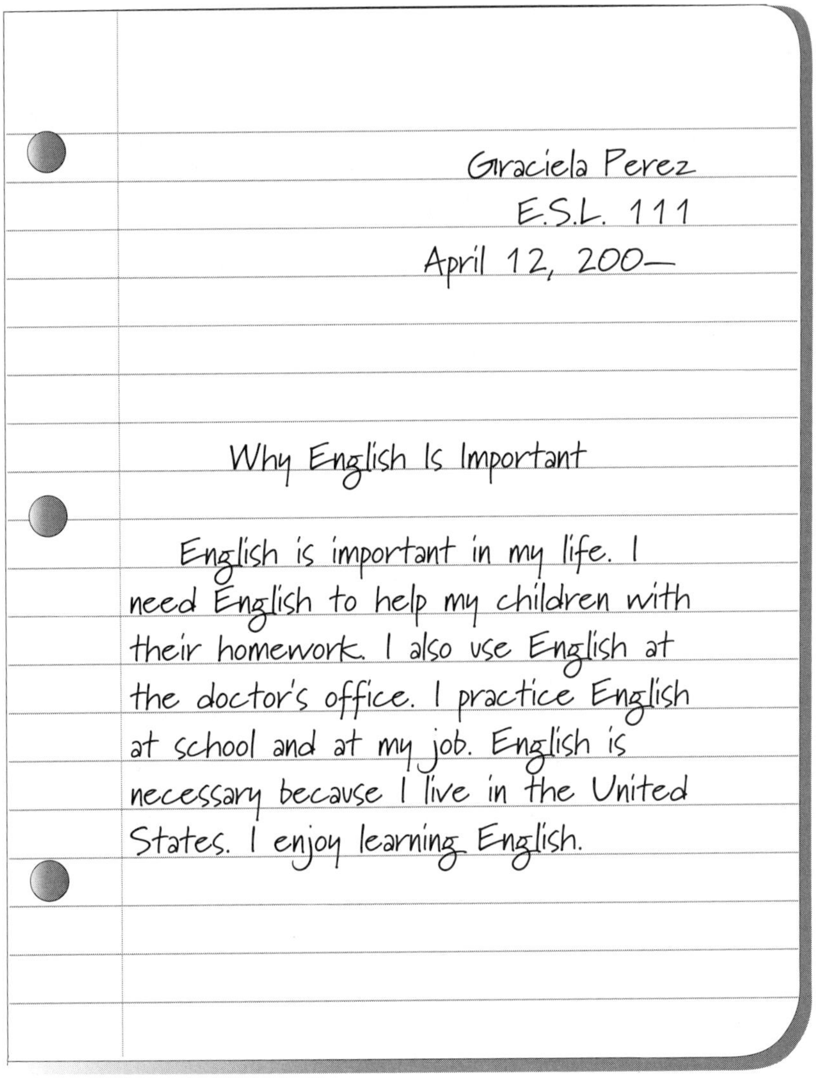

Graciela Perez
E.S.L. 111
April 12, 200—

Why English Is Important

   English is important in my life. I need English to help my children with their homework. I also use English at the doctor's office. I practice English at school and at my job. English is necessary because I live in the United States. I enjoy learning English.

serious	studious
three-ring binder	notebook
useful	practical

Comprehension

▶**EXERCISE 5** **Listen to your teacher read the sentences. Repeat the sentences after your teacher. Then write T (true) or F (false) for each statement.**

_____ 1. English is useful at home, work, and school.

_____ 2. English is not important in the United States.

_____ 3. English is necessary for a job.

_____ 4. All people listen to English on the radio.

_____ 5. Some immigrants study English at school.

_____ 6. At school, do not be serious.

_____ 7. It is important to prepare for classes.

_____ 8. Study before a test.

_____ 9. When you are absent, call another student or the teacher.

_____ 10. Hardworking students are not on time to class every day.

▶**EXERCISE 6** **Write the letter of the phrase that completes each sentence.**

1. Many immigrants __c_____   a. by watching TV in English.

2. English is important _____   b. for many reasons.

3. It is necessary to study and take _____   c. are in the United States.

4. Listen to the teachers and _____   d. materials to class.

5. Make an appointment _____   e. use a pen.

6. It is important _____   f. ask questions.

7. When you do homework _____   g. with a tutor.

8. Some people learn English _____   h. to prepare for class at home.

▶**EXERCISE 7** **Read the questions and answer them orally with your teacher. Then answer the questions orally with a classmate. At home, write the answers for homework. Answer in complete sentences.**

1. Where are you from? _____

   _____

2. What language do you speak? _____

   _____

3. Where is it important for you to use English? _____

   _____

4. Do you ask questions in class? _____

   _____

5. When do you study at home? _____

   _____

6. Is English necessary for your job? _____

   _____

7. Do you use English after class? _____

   _____

8. What materials do you take to class? _____

   _____

9. Why is homework important? _____

   _____

10. Do you read, watch TV, or listen to the radio in English? _____

    _____

Vocabulary Practice

▶**EXERCISE 8** **Complete each sentence with a word from the box.**

class	dictionaries	doctor	emergency	home
homework	immigrant	materials	problem	question
streets	tutor	ways	work	

1. I speak English with my supervisor at _____.

2. A person who is new to a country is an _____.

3. I always take my _____ to class. I take paper, a pencil, and a notebook.

4. We study English at _____ after dinner.

5. There are many _____ to practice English.

6. I go to my _____ every day at the university.

7. If I don't understand a word, I ask the teacher a _____.

8. I need to speak English with my _____ at the medical clinic.

9. I go to the doctor's office when I have a medical _____.

10. I call 911 in an _____.

11. Students look for new words in _____.

12. The _____ in my neighborhood are very safe. There is no crime.

13. If a class is too difficult for me, I see a _____ at school.

14. I write my _____ with a pen.

Reading Charts and Graphs

▶EXERCISE 9

A. Study the chart about English speakers and speakers of other languages in the United States.

Language use and English ability by speakers of other languages 5 years of age and over

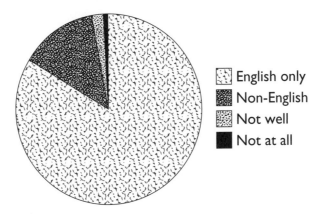

☐ English only
▨ Non-English
▨ Not well
■ Not at all

Total population, 262,375,152; English only, 215,423,557; non-English, 45,951,595; included in total non-English: not well, 7,620,719; not at all, 3,366,132.

Source: U.S. Census Bureau, 2000

B. Answer the questions about the pie graph.

1. How many people do not speak English at all? _____

2. Do many Americans speak only English? How many? _____

3. For which groups are ESL classes a good idea? _____

Reading 2   The Dictionary

Before You Read

▶**EXERCISE 10** Scan (read quickly) the reading for the words that mean the *opposite* (antonyms) of the following words.

a. not practical _____

b. show _____

c. boring _____

▶**EXERCISE 11** Answer these questions.

1. What information do we learn from a dictionary? _____

_____

2. The main idea (the most important idea) of each paragraph is underlined. What is the main idea of the first paragraph? Write it here: _____

_____

Words from the Reading*

alphabetical order	spell checker
definition	spelling
part of speech	useful
pronunciation	

*Your teacher can help you understand these words and others listed at the end of the chapter and on the Web site at http://esl.college.hmco.com/students

---

Read to find out why a dictionary is useful and helpful.

⌒ The Dictionary

We need helpful materials, especially a dictionary, when we take a class. <u>A dictionary is fun, interesting, and very useful when we study a new language.</u> Students can use a regular paper dictionary or an electronic dictionary. Computers also have a spell checker that students can use when they write homework papers. When we use a dictionary, we learn new vocabulary. Dictionaries also provide pronunciation guides, spelling, parts of speech, and definitions.

A dictionary is very practical when you study at home. During class, don't **hide** in the dictionary! **Pay attention** to the class. Also it is a good idea to use the dictionary the second time we read something. The first time we read it, many times we **guess,** or think we understand, the definition of some words without the dictionary.

A dictionary shows us helpful information about each word. Study the parts of these three entries, which are in alphabetical order.

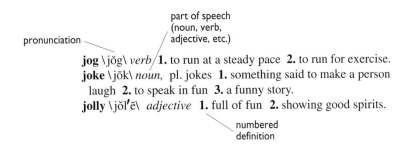

The letters and marks between the \ \ (slashes) or [ ] (brackets) show the pronunciation of the word. The word after the slashes or brackets is the part of speech (noun, verb, adjective, etc.). The part of speech helps us to use the words correctly in a sentence. Then there are one or more numbered definitions.

A dictionary is an excellent tool for spelling and writing and also helpful for pronunciation.

guess	predict; give an opinion
hide	conceal; cover
pay attention	concentrate; be alert

 Comprehension

►**EXERCISE 12** **Write the letter of the phrase that completes the sentence.**

1. The letters between \ \ are _____ 　　a. alphabetical order.

2. The noun, verb, and adjective are _____ 　　b. you study.

3. There are one or more _____ 　　c. the pronunciation.

4. The words in the dictionary are in _____ 　　d. the part of speech.

5. The dictionary is important when _____ 　　e. definitions.

▶**EXERCISE 13** **Read the sentence, then write T (true) or F (false).**

_____ 1. There are no definitions in a dictionary.

_____ 2. There is no pronunciation in a dictionary.

_____ 3. A dictionary is excellent for spelling.

_____ 4. Nouns, verbs, and adjectives are parts of speech.

_____ 5. A dictionary is useful the second time we read something.

_____ 6. Alphabetical means A to Z order.

▶**EXERCISE 14** **Study the words from the dictionary, then answer the questions.**

grade	215	_grammar_

grade \grād\ _noun,_ pl. grades **1.** a mark for the quality of school work **2.** a class or year in school.
graduate \grăj'ōō-āt\ _verb_ **1.** to complete school **2.** to get a diploma or degree.
grammar \grăm'ər\ _noun_ **1.** the study of words in a sentence **2.** the rules for using words in a sentence.

1. What is one definition for graduate? _to complete school_

2. What part of speech are _grade_ and _grammar?_ _____

3. What part of speech is _graduate?_ _____

4. What order are _grade, graduate,_ and _grammar_ in? _____

5. Which word has the definition "a mark for the quality of school work"?

_____

6. Which word has the definition "the study of words in a sentence"?

_____

Vocabulary Practice

▶EXERCISE 15 **Complete each sentence with a word from the box.**

| book | classes | date | friends | homework | hospital | letter | materials |

1. My two _____ are students at City College.

2. English is important in the emergency room at the _____.

3. My English _____ are interesting.

4. Our teacher gives us homework from the _____.

5. My _____ is sometimes difficult.

6. My _____ for school are a pencil, paper, and books.

7. The _____ today is September 7, 2005.

8. The _____ from my son's teacher is in English.

▶EXERCISE 16 **Complete each sentence with a word from the box.**

Prefixes: *pre-* and *re-*

The prefixes pre- (before) and re- (again) change the meaning of a word.

  preview = view (look at) before
  review = view (look at) again

Before you read, *preview* the vocabulary.
After you read, *review* the vocabulary.

| preheat | preschool | reorganize | repeat | reread |

1. _____ the oven before you make the pizza.

2. Before kindergarten, children go to _____.

3. You need to read that again. It's a good idea to _____ it.

4. Can you say that again please? Can you please _____ that word?

5. You need to organize your papers again. You have to _____ them.

Expansion Activities

▶ **Activity 1 Record Homework Contacts** *When good students are sick, they call other students to ask for the homework. Ask three students in the class for their name and phone number. Write them here:*

_____

Name   Phone Number

_____

Name   Phone Number

_____

Name   Phone Number

▶ **Activity 2 Practice a Message for Your Teacher** *Practice leaving a message on your teacher's phone. Also write the information below.*

1. Complete the message in writing.

2. Practice saying the message to a partner.

3. Say the message to the class.

4. Call your teacher and leave the message.

My teacher's phone number: _____

Hello Mr./Mrs./Ms. _____. My name is _____.
                            your teacher's name   your name
I am in your _____ class on _____ at _____.
                   name of class   days   time of class
Today is _____. I am sick today, so I won't be in class. Thank you.
                  day

▶ **Activity 3 Write a Short Letter in English**

Complete a letter to your child's teacher. You may use the words in parentheses or words of your own choice.

Dear Mr./Mrs./Ms. _____,

My son/daughter _____ needs help with homework in _____.
                          child's name   school subject
He/she needs _____ (a tutor, extra help after school, organization of ideas).

I want to _____ (meet with you, help in the classroom, visit your

class).

_____
your name

Vocabulary List

Adjectives

necessary

recent

three-ring

useful

Adverb

often

Nouns

appointment

binder

book

cartoon

date

dictionary /
dictionaries

emergency /
emergencies

entry / entries

eraser

grade

home

homework

hospital

letter

material

medicine

news

paper

pen

preschool

problem

question

street

telephone

tutor

Verbs

ask

attend

communicate

enjoy

get

guess

has / have

hide

keep

learn

miss

need

pay attention

prefer

preheat

preview

reorganize

repeat

reread

review

watch

**Dictionary
Terms**

alphabetical
order

definition

parts of speech

pronunciation

spelling

If you want to review vocabulary and complete additional activities related to this unit, go to the Read to Succeed 1 Web site at http://esl.college.hmco.com/students

CHAPTER 5

I Don't Have Time!

Reading 1 "Ana's Busy Life"

Before You Read

▶**EXERCISE 1** Discuss these questions with a partner or a small group.

1. Do you have a problem with time?

2. Do you have too many activities?

3. Do you have a plan for your time each week?

▶EXERCISE 2 Match the letter of the pictures with the correct sentences.

A.

B.

C.

D.

E.

1. The family has a very busy life. _____

2. The mother is a college student. _____

3. The husband is not happy that Ana is a student. _____

4. Ana is a cashier at a supermarket. _____

5. She cooks and helps with the homework. _____

▶**EXERCISE 3** **Scan (look over) the reading and answer questions 1–7. Then answer general questions 8–12 based on your knowledge.**

1. Where does a homemaker work? _____

2. What is one of your goals? _____

3. What is something that people quit? _____

4. What is the title of the reading? _____

5. What is Ana's problem? _____

   _____

6. What is the solution for Ana? _____

   _____

7. The main idea of the second paragraph is <u>underlined</u>. What is the main idea of the first paragraph? Find it and write it here. _____

   _____

8. What activities does a college student have? _____

   _____

9. A cashier works at a supermarket. True or false? _____

10. Are some married women students? _____

    _____

11. A person can quit a job, school, or a job. True or false? _____

12. The opposite of realistic is unrealistic. True or false? _____

Words from the Reading*

busy   unhappy
spend time

*Your teacher can help you understand these words and others listed at the end of the chapter and on the Web site at http://esl.college.hmco.com/students

Read about a typical student's schedule.

"Ana's Busy Life"

I just don't have time for everything—family, school, work, and exercise. I have to go to work, and I have two tests tomorrow!

Ana, will you have time to cook tonight?

I want to go to the pizza place.

Ana Garcia is a very busy person. She is a mother, a wife, a student, a **homemaker,** and a supermarket cashier. She cooks breakfast for her family in the morning. She helps the children with homework in the afternoon. She prepares dinner for the family in the evening before work. Ana is also a full-time ESL student from 9:00 a.m. to 1:30 p.m. She also works 35 hours a week as a cashier at night at a supermarket. Ana has four children and a husband. It is difficult to take classes, work full-time, take care of her children, be a homemaker, spend time with her husband, and study for her classes. Ana's husband is unhappy that his wife is a student. Ana wants to continue her classes. Her goal at school is a degree in computers. She has to make time for all her activities.

Ana is very intelligent, but <u>she has a problem with her schedule and time</u>. She has too many classes, and she doesn't have time for all her activities. Ana is always tired, and she doesn't have time for all her homework. She does not have time to relax or to exercise. Her husband and children also say they never see her. She has to plan her week and write a **realistic** schedule for next semester. Her schedule is not **realistic** now because she has too many activities. Ana has to plan for all her important activities. She thinks four classes are too many for her. Next semester, she wants only two classes. She is a very good student and wants a career in computers. She does not want to **quit** school.

homemaker	housewife
quit	stop
realistic	real; practical

Comprehension

▶**EXERCISE 4** **Write T (true) or F (false) for each statement.**

_____ 1. Ana Garcia is not very busy.

_____ 2. Ana studies, works, and has a family.

_____ 3. It is easy to work, study, and have a family.

_____ 4. Ana's husband is happy she is a student.

_____ 5. Ana has to make time for her important activities.

_____ 6. Ana has no problems with her schedule.

_____ 7. A realistic schedule doesn't have too many activities.

_____ 8. Ana doesn't want a career.

_____ 9. Ana Garcia wants to quit school.

_____ 10. Her husband wants Ana to be at home.

▶**EXERCISE 5** **Read the questions and answer them orally with your teacher. Then answer the questions orally with a classmate. At home, write the answers for homework. Answer in complete sentences.**

1. What are the hours Ana is at school? _____

_____

2. How many hours a week does she work? _____

_____

3. How many children does she have? _____

_____

4. What is her problem? _____

_____

5. What career does she want? _____

_____

►**EXERCISE 6** **Discuss the questions with a partner, then write the answers.**

Questions with *why*

Why asks about a reason.	**Answer with *because.* . . .**
Why are you a student?	*I am a student because I want to learn.*

1. Why does Ana have a problem? *Ana has a problem because she has too many activities.*

2. Why does she work 35 hours a week? _____

_____

3. Why is Ana a student? _____

_____

4. Why is her husband unhappy? _____

_____

5. Why is a realistic schedule a good idea for Ana? _____

_____

6. Why do you think the children are unhappy with Ana's schedule? _____

_____

7. Why are all of Ana's activities difficult for her? _____

_____

8. Why does Ana only want two classes next semester? _____

_____

9. Why do you think Ana wants to study computers after ESL classes? _____

_____

10. Why is a career important (or not important) for a woman? _____

_____

📖 Vocabulary Practice

▶**EXERCISE 7** Complete each sentence with a word from the box.

activities	career	goal	husband
problem	quit	schedule	time

1. Ana wants a _____ in computers.

2. She has a _____ with time.

3. Ana has to make time for all her _____.

4. She needs a realistic _____.

5. She does not want to _____ school.

6. Her problem is _____.

7. Ana's _____ is a career in computers.

8. Her _____ is unhappy that she is a student.

▶**EXERCISE 8** Complete the paragraph with words from the box. You may use the words more than once.

has	is	plan	quit	wants	works

Ana _____ a very busy person. She _____ a full-time student. She also _____ as a cashier at a supermarket. Ana _____ four children and a husband. It _____ difficult to work, study, and have a family. Her husband _____ unhappy that his wife _____ a student. Ana _____ a problem with time. She has to _____ a realistic schedule. She _____ a career in computers and does not want to _____ school.

► **EXERCISE 9** **Complete the sentences with words from the box.**

Prefixes: *un-* and *dis-*
The prefixes un- (not) and dis- (not) change the meaning of a word.
unhappy = not happy   *Ana's husband is unhappy.*
dislike = not like   *I dislike some vegetables.*

unlimited	unpopular	unrealistic	untrue
disconnected	dishonest	disorganized	

1. Her schedule is _____. Her schedule is *not* realistic.

2. That idea isn't popular. It's _____.

3. That's false. It's _____.

4. There are so many opportunities. The opportunities are _____.

5. My papers aren't organized. They are _____.

6. My friend isn't _____. He's honest.

7. The phone is never connected. It is always _____.

Reading Charts and Graphs

▶**EXERCISE 10**

A. Study the bar graph about how much education adults have.

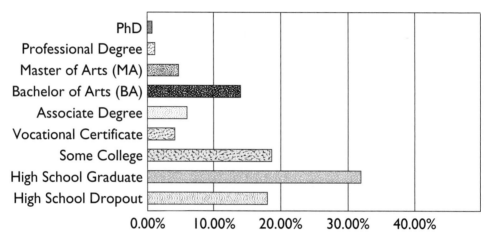

How Much Education Adults Have (18+ years old)

PhD, 0.8%; professional degree, 1.2%; master of arts, 4.8%; bachelor of arts, 14.1%; associate degree, 6.1%; vocational certificate, 4.2%; some college, 18.7%; high school graduate, 32%; high school dropout, 18.1%.

Source: U.S. Department of Commerce, 2001

B. Answer the questions about the bar graph.

1. What is the percentage of high school dropouts? _____

2. What is the percentage of associate degrees? _____

3. What percentage of people have a bachelor of arts degree? _____

4. What degree or certificate do you want? _____

Reading 2   A Realistic Schedule

Before You Read

▶**EXERCISE 11** Discuss these questions with a partner or a small group.

1. What is an activity that people do for relaxation?

2. People waste water when they take long showers. What is another thing that people waste?

3. What is something that you do at the last minute?

4. What activities are in your schedule?

5. Do you have a realistic schedule?

6. The main idea of this reading is the last sentence of the paragraph. Write it here.

_____

Words from the Reading*

calendar book   relaxation

exercise   shopping

*Your teacher can help you understand these words and
 others listed at the end of the chapter and on the Web
 site at http://esl.college.hmco.com/students

Read about realistic schedules.

   Some students have a plan and calendar book for their activities. They write down their classes, work schedule, homework time, meals, family activities, exercise time, sleep time, and relaxation time. They never take too many classes. Other students have a schedule, but it is not realistic. They have too little time and too many activities. They do not plan for all their activities and do not have a good schedule. They have classes, but they do not plan for homework time. Some students **waste time** and have to study for tests **at the last minute.** Students need to have time for class, work, family, friends, recreation, sleeping, eating, shopping, exercising, and studying. It is important for busy students to have a realistic schedule and to make time for all their important activities.

at the last minute	very late
waste time	not use time well

Comprehension

▶**EXERCISE 12** **Write T (true) or F (false) for each statement.**

_____ 1. Many students only have a little time.

_____ 2. All students plan for all their activities.

_____ 3. All students have a realistic schedule.

_____ 4. Some students waste time.

_____ 5. All students study for tests at the last minute.

_____ 6. A realistic schedule is necessary.

_____ 7. Students have to make time for important activities.

▶**EXERCISE 13** **Read the questions and answer them orally with your teacher. Then answer the questions orally with a classmate. At home, write the answers for homework. Answer in complete sentences.**

A. About You

1. How many classes do you have? _____

_____

2. What hours do you work, either at home or on the job or both? _____

_____

3. Do you plan for all your activities? _____

_____

4. Do you plan for study time each week? _____

_____

5. What is your number 1 problem? _____

_____

B. General Questions

1. Does a married person have more activities? _____

_____

2. Is it good for a wife to take classes? _____

_____

3. Is a career important for a woman? _____

_____

4. How does the family feel when a parent is a student? _____

_____

5. Do you want a career? If so, why? _____

_____

Vocabulary Practice

▶**EXERCISE 14** **Turn back to the reading about realistic schedules on page 79. Find the antonym, or opposite, for each __underlined__ word.**

1. They <u>always</u> study late. _____

2. I have <u>too much</u> time. _____

3. Watching television is <u>unimportant</u>. _____

4. My <u>first</u> class is at 8:00 a.m. _____

5. <u>None</u> of my friends speak English. _____

6. Planning to win the Lotto is <u>unrealistic</u>. _____

7. I have only a <u>few</u> friends. _____

8. I have a <u>bad</u> schedule this term. _____

Grammar Hints: Present Tense

▶**EXERCISE 15** **Look at Ana's schedule. Then complete each sentence with a present tense verb.**

Subject Pronouns and Present Tense Verbs

Singular
I do / I think
you do / you think
he, she does / he, she thinks

Plural
we do / we think
you do / you think
they do / they think

Examples:
Ana works at night. She needs a good schedule. (affirmative)
Ana doesn't relax. She doesn't play a sport. (negative)
Does Ana work? Does she always study? (interrogative)

Ana's schedule
Monday through Friday:
6:00–8:00 a.m.: Wake up; feed and get kids ready for school
8:00–8:40 a.m.: Take kids to school

9:00 a.m.–1:30 p.m.: Business classes
2:00–3:00 p.m.: Pick up kids after school
3:00–4:00 p.m.: Help with kids homework and snacks
4:00–5:00 p.m.: Cook dinner
5:30–11:30 p.m.: Work at the supermarket
12:00–1:30 a.m.: Study
1:00–6:00 a.m.: Sleep

1. Ana _____ at 6:00 a.m.

2. She _____ the children to school at 8:00.

3. Ana does not _____ a good schedule.

4. Her husband does not _____ Ana to go to school.

5. Ana _____ her children from school at about 2:00 p.m.

6. Does Ana _____ the children with homework?

7. She _____ dinner between 4:00 and 5:00.

8. Ana _____ very late between 12:00 and 1:30 a.m.

Expansion Activities

▶ **Activity 1 Time Flies** *Write a schedule for the week. Plan for classes, job, eating, cleaning the house, recreation, exercising, family, shopping, friends, sleeping, and studying.*

	Sunday	Monday	Tuesday	Wednesday	Thursday	Friday	Saturday
7:00 AM							
8:00 AM							
9:00 AM							
10:00 AM							
11:00 AM							
12:00 PM							
1:00 PM							
2:00 PM							
3:00 PM							
4:00 PM							
5:00 PM							
6:00 PM							
7:00 PM							
8:00 PM							
9:00 PM							
10:00 PM							
11:00 PM							

▶ **Activity 2 Where Does the Day Go?** *Look at how Pam spends her school day. Then make a chart for how you spend your school day.*

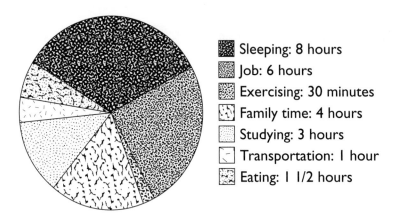

Sleeping: 8 hours
Job: 6 hours
Exercising: 30 minutes
Family time: 4 hours
Studying: 3 hours
Transportation: 1 hour
Eating: 1 1/2 hours

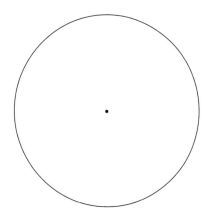

► **Activity 3 Time to Relax** *It is important to have time to relax. Some people exercise to relax. Other people read books or watch TV. Interview five people from your class. Ask them this question: What do you do to relax? Then write about them.*

Examples:

My friend Martha reads magazines in her free time. Three of my classmates watch TV for relaxation. Ho-Sik plays the guitar to relax.

_____

_____

_____

_____

_____

_____

_____

_____

_____

_____

_____

Vocabulary List

Adjectives

disconnected

dishonest

disorganized

first

little

realistic

unimportant

unlimited

unpopular

unrealistic

untrue

Adverbs

always

Nouns

activity / activities

book

calendar

children

eating

education

exercise

exercising

goal

homemaker

housewife / housewives

percentage

recreation

relaxation

schedule

shopping

sleeping

solution

studying

time

week

Preposition

of

Pronoun

Verbs

dislike

exercise

help

make

plan

quit

think

want

waste

Expressions

at the last minute

spend time

too much

waste time

If you want to review vocabulary and complete additional activities related to this unit, go to the Read to Succeed 1 Web site at http://esl.college.hmco.com/students

Survival and Culture

Woman's Community Shelter

Family Physicians

Happy New Year

CHAPTER 6

An Appointment with the Doctor

Reading I   A Bigger Family for the Itos

Before You Read

▶**EXERCISE I** Discuss these questions with a partner or a small group.

1. When do people see a doctor?

2. If you are sick in your native country, do you visit a pharmacy, drugstore, or a doctor first? Can a pharmacy sell you medicines without a prescription?

3. What can you buy at a drugstore in the United States? Can you buy prescription medicines, cream, or candy there?

4. Is medical insurance expensive or cheap?

▶**EXERCISE 2** **Listen to your teacher read each sentence. Say the sentences after your teacher. Then match each sentence with the correct picture.**

A.

B.

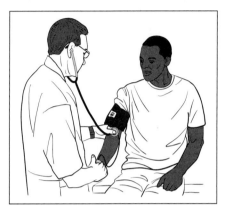

C.

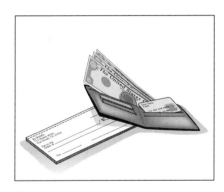

D.

E.

1. Please complete the health history. _____

2. Hiroko is pregnant. _____

3. Please read and sign your name. _____

4. "Let's take your blood pressure." _____

5. Cash, check, or credit card? _____

▶**EXERCISE 3** **Scan (read quickly) the reading for the following words. Guess what they mean without using a dictionary. Write your guess on the line.**

1. pregnant _____

2. health history _____

3. sign _____

▶**EXERCISE 4** **Answer these questions.**

1. What is the title of the reading? _____

2. What do you think the reading is about? _____

    _____

3. Why is Hiroko at the doctor's office? _____

    _____

Words from the Reading*

health history	waiting room
medical insurance	yet
receptionist	

*Your teacher can help you understand these words and others listed at the end of the chapter and on the Web site at http://esl.college.hmco.com/students

---

Read about Hiroko's appointment with the doctor.

⌒ A Bigger Family for the Itos

Hiroko Ito has an important appointment with Dr. Maria Perez today. She arrives at 2:50 p.m., and her appointment is at 3:00. She does not want to arrive late. Hiroko does not know for sure, but she thinks that she is **pregnant.** Hiroko and her husband do not have any children yet, so they are very happy. This is going to be their first child, and they are **excited.** Hiroko and her husband want three children. They don't have medical insurance.

"May I help you?" says the receptionist.

"Yes, please. I have an appointment with Dr. Perez," says Hiroko.

"Please sit down and complete this health history," says the receptionist. Ten minutes later, Hiroko **returns** the health history to the receptionist.

"Please read the paper and **sign** your name," says the receptionist. "Do you have insurance?"

"No, I don't have any medical insurance," answers Hiroko.

"Cash, check, or credit card is fine," the receptionist tells her.

"I want a payment plan. I want to pay a little each month," says Hiroko.
"Do you want us to bill you for this visit?" asks the receptionist.
"Yes, please send the bill to my house," Hiroko says.
"Please wait in the waiting room," the receptionist tells her.

excited	enthusiastic
pregnant	going to have a baby
return	give back
sign	write your name

Comprehension

►**EXERCISE 5** **Write T (true) or F (false) for each statement.**

_____ 1. Hiroko Ito has a doctor's appointment today.

_____ 2. Her appointment is at 3:30.

_____ 3. She thinks she has heart problems.

_____ 4. Hiroko and her husband are very happy.

_____ 5. They want five children.

_____ 6. The name of the doctor is Hiroko.

_____ 7. Hiroko has to read the paper and sign the paper.

_____ 8. Hiroko and her husband have health insurance.

_____ 9. Hiroko wants a payment plan.

_____ 10. Hiroko waits in the waiting room for the doctor.

▶**EXERCISE 6** **Read the questions and answer them orally with your teacher. Then answer the questions orally with a classmate. At home, write the answers for homework. Answer in complete sentences.**

1. At what time does Hiroko arrive? _____

_____

2. What time is her appointment? _____

_____

3. What is the name of her doctor? _____

_____

4. What does Hiroko think about herself? _____

_____

5. How many children do Hiroko and her husband have? _____

_____

6. How many children do they want? _____

_____

7. What does Hiroko need to complete? _____

_____

8. What does Hiroko sign? _____

_____

9. What health insurance do Hiroko and her husband have? _____

_____

10. What plan does Hiroko want to use to pay the doctor? _____

_____

Why-questions:

1. Why is Hiroko at the doctor's? *Hiroko is at the doctor's because she is pregnant.*

2. Why are Hiroko and her husband happy and excited? _____

3. Why is the health history necessary? _____

4. Why is health insurance important? _____

5. Why does Hiroko want a payment plan? _____

Vocabulary Practice

▶**EXERCISE 7** **Your teacher will pronounce each word. Repeat each word. If it is about Hiroko's medical exam, say yes and circle the word. If it is not, say no.**

(appointment)	health insurance	pregnant
diet	heart problem	reading
disease	no alcohol	receptionist
doctor	no drugs	sign the paper
doctor bill	payment plan	waiting room
health history	physical exam	

►**EXERCISE 8** **Pronounce the words in the box after your teacher. Then complete each sentence with the correct word from the box.**

Negatives in Present Tense

Singular	Plural
I/you/we/they + don't + verb	He/she/it + doesn't + verb

credit	doesn't have	don't have	excited	fine
first	health	payment	return	waiting

1. Hiroko and her husband are very _____.

2. This is their _____ child.

3. They _____ any children.

4. Hiroko needs to _____ the health history to the receptionist.

5. Hiroko _____ an appointment tonight.

6. The receptionist says to wait in the _____ room.

7. Hiroko does not use a _____ card.

8. Hiroko and her husband do not have _____ insurance.

9. The receptionist says, "Cash, check, or credit card is _____."

10. Hiroko wants a _____ plan at the doctor's office.

►**EXERCISE 9** **Write the opposite expression or word.**

1. unimportant _____

2. late _____

3. stand up _____

4. last _____

5. Yes, I do. _____

▶**EXERCISE 10** **Write the short command.**

1. The nurse wants Hiroko to sit down on the table.

    "Please _____*sit down*_____ on the table," the nurse says.

2. The nurse wants Hiroko to complete the health history.

    "Please _____ the health history," she says.

3. The receptionist wants Hiroko to sign her name on the paper.

    "Please _____ your name," the receptionist says.

4. The medical assistant wants Hiroko to read the paragraph.

    "Please _____ it," she says.

5. She wants Hiroko to wait in the waiting room.

    "Please _____ in there," she says.

6. The doctor wants Hiroko to make another appointment.

    "Please _____ another appointment," she says.

7. Dr. Perez wants Hiroko to take these vitamins.

    "Please _____ these vitamins," the doctor says.

8. The doctor doesn't want Hiroko to work too much.

    "Please don't _____ too much," she says.

9. The doctor says not to drink alcohol.

    "Do not _____ alcohol," Dr. Perez says.

10. The doctor says to come back next month.

    "_____ back next month," the doctor says.

Reading Charts and Graphs

►EXERCISE 11

A. Study the graph about children and health insurance.

All Children 18 Years of Age or Less with *No* Health Insurance in United States in 1996

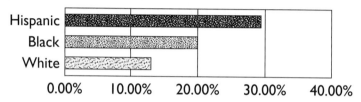

In 1996, 10.6 million children (14.8% of all children) had no
health insurance. Percentages (%) of children with no health
insurance by ethnic group for 1996 are White, 13.9%; Black,
18.8%; and Hispanic, 28.9%. (In 1987, 8.2 million children were
without health insurance.)

Source: U.S. Dept. of Commerce, 1998

B. Answer the questions about the chart and the other statistics.

1. How many children did not have health insurance in the United States in 1987?

   _____

2. How many children did not have health insurance in 1996? Did the number
   go up? _____

3. What percentage of White children did not have health insurance in 1996?

   _____

4. What percentage of Hispanic children did not have health insurance in 1996?

   _____

Reading 2   The Physical Examination

Before You Read

▶**EXERCISE 12 Answer the following questions in a complete sentence.**

1. What is your height in inches? _____

   _____

2. What is a normal temperature for a person? _____

   _____

3. Do you have normal blood pressure? _____

   _____

4. What is your weight in pounds? (1 pound is 2.2 kilos.) _____

   _____

5. What are examples of jewelry? _____

   _____

6. Do you have a physical examination every year? _____

   _____

▶**EXERCISE 13 Scan the reading below. Then answer these questions.**

1. Where is Hiroko's physical exam? _____

2. Who is the doctor? _____

3. What tests are necessary? _____

4. What does Hiroko hope? _____

   _____

5. What are five things you can buy at a drugstore in the United States? _____

   _____

6. What are carrots, tomatoes, and lettuce examples of? _____

   _____

Words from the Reading*

blood pressure	protein
blood test	robe
jewelry	symptom
laugh	temperature
prenatal	waiting room
prescription	whole grains

*Your teacher can help you understand these words and others listed at the end of the chapter and on the Web site at http://esl.college.hmco.com/students

Read about Hiroko's physical examination.

The Physical Examination

Hiroko is nervous about her physical examination. Hiroko hopes that she is pregnant. The nurse comes to the waiting room and says, "Mrs. Ito? Please come with me. I want to check your **weight,** temperature, and **height.** Then I will show you to the examination room."

Hiroko begins her physical examination with the nurse. "Please sit here for a blood pressure and temperature check," says the nurse. "Then take off all your **clothing** and jewelry. Please put on this robe and sit on the table. After the examination, you will have a blood test in the lab. The doctor is ready for you now."

Dr. Perez comes in the room and says hello to Hiroko. The doctor listens to Hiroko's symptoms. Hiroko says she is always tired and sleepy, and she does not have any energy. She also feels **nauseated** in the morning. The doctor says she is probably pregnant, but a blood test is necessary to make sure.

Dr. Perez asks, "Do you eat well?"

Hiroko says, "Yes, I eat fruit and vegetables every day."

The doctor recommends eating whole grains, **plenty** of fruits and vegetables, proteins, and milk, cheese, or yogurt. "Also," says the doctor, "take this prescription for vitamins to a pharmacy. Get it filled once a month. Now, do you have any questions for me?"

"I have many questions, Dr. Perez," laughs Hiroko, "but for now, I have two. First, should my husband come with me to these visits?"

"Yes, if it is possible for him," answers the doctor.

"Are there prenatal classes for me?" Hiroko asks.

"Yes, here is some information about classes for you and your husband to read at home. And here's a schedule of prenatal classes."

Dr. Perez reminds Hiroko to call her office if she has any questions or problems. Finally, Dr. Perez tells her to make another appointment for next month.

clothing	clothes
height	how tall a person is
nauseated	wanting to vomit
plenty	a lot
weight	how heavy a person is

 Comprehension

▶**EXERCISE 14** **Write T (true) or F (false) for each statement.**

_____ 1. Hiroko has a dental exam with Dr. Perez.

_____ 2. The nurse checks her weight and appetite.

_____ 3. The nurse takes Hiroko to the operating room.

_____ 4. Hiroko has a blood pressure and temperature check.

_____ 5. Hiroko takes off her clothing and jewelry.

_____ 6. She puts on a beautiful dress.

_____ 7. She has a blood test in the waiting room.

_____ 8. The doctor says Hiroko is probably pregnant.

_____ 9. Hiroko doesn't have any symptoms.

_____ 10. The doctor gives Hiroko a prescription for medicine.

▶**EXERCISE 15** **Read the questions and answer them orally with your teacher. Then answer the questions orally with a classmate. At home, write the answers for homework. Answer in a complete sentence.**

1. Who comes to the waiting room for Hiroko? _____

_____

2. What does the nurse check first? _____

_____

3. Where does the nurse take Hiroko next? _____

_____

4. What does the nurse check in the examination room? _____

_____

5. What does Hiroko take off? _____

_____

6. What does she put on? _____

_____

7. Where is the blood test? _____

_____

8. When is the blood test? _____

_____

9. Who listens to Hiroko's symptoms? _____

_____

10. Where does Hiroko need to take the prescription for vitamins? _____

_____

Why questions:

1. Why is Hiroko nervous? _Hiroko is nervous because she is pregnant._ _____

_____

2. Why does Hiroko need prenatal classes? _____

_____

3. Why is a blood test necessary? _____

_____

4. Why does Dr. Perez think Hiroko is pregnant? _____

_____

5. Why are vitamins good for Hiroko? _____

_____

Vocabulary Practice

▶**EXERCISE 16** **Your teacher will pronounce each command. If it is a medical command about Hiroko's medical exam, say yes and circle the command. If it is not, say no.**

(Please come with me.)	Put on this gown.	Quit school.
Study English.	Sit on the table.	Take off your jewelry.
Take off your clothing.	Don't smoke.	Take these vitamins.
Write a schedule.	Don't take drugs.	Make another appointment.
Transfer to the university.	Sit here.	Take a blood test.
Don't use alcohol.	Put on this hat.	Sit on the floor.

▶**EXERCISE 17** **Complete each sentence with a word from the box.**

another	feels nauseated	fill	nervous
next	physical	ready	tired

1. Hiroko has an appointment _____ month.

2. She is _____ about her physical examination.

3. Hiroko says she is always _____.

4. She _____ in the morning.

5. Her _____ examination is at 3:00.

6. You need to _____ this prescription at a pharmacy.

7. Dr. Perez is _____ for Hiroko's examination.

8. She has _____ appointment in June.

Grammar Hints: Object Pronouns

▶**EXERCISE 18** **Change the underlined noun in each sentence to a pronoun.**

Singular		**Plural**	
me	See **me** next month	us	Call **us** tomorrow.
you	She wants **you** to exercise.	you	I will see **you** for the test.
him, her, it	Sign **it**, please.	them	Take **them** once a day.

1. Take the vitamins every day.

   Take _____*them*_____ every day.

2. Make the appointment for next month.

   Make _____ for next month.

3. Listen to Dr. Maria Perez.

   Listen to _____.

4. Ask <u>Mr. Jones</u> about the information.

   Ask _____ about the information.

5. Complete <u>the health history</u>, please.

   Complete _____, please.

6. Bring <u>the children</u>, please.

   Bring _____, please.

7. Don't waste <u>the money</u>.

   Don't waste _____.

8. Give <u>the health forms</u> to the receptionist, please.

   Give _____ to the receptionist, please.

 # Expansion Activities

▶ **Activity 1 Call the Doctor!** *With a partner, write the dialogue for a phone call to the doctor or dentist to make an appointment. Explain why you want to see the doctor. Then practice the dialogue and present it to the class.*

▶ **Activity 2 What to Do?** *Hiroko's friend Gina is 19 years old. Gina is two months pregnant, but she is not married. Her boyfriend doesn't have a job. He says he loves Gina, but he is not ready to be a father. Gina doesn't know whether she is ready to be a mother. Talk with your classmates about possible solutions for Gina. What is good for her? For her boyfriend? For the baby? What services are there to help her decide? Write your answers to these questions and discuss them with a partner or a small group.*

Vocabulary List

Adjectives

another
credit
fine
last
nauseated
nervous
next
physical
pregnant
prenatal
ready
sleepy
ten
tired
whole

Demonstrative Adjective

these

Adverbs

down
finally
later
probably
yet

Conjunctions

and
but
whether

Nouns

alcohol
bill
blood
blood pressure
blood test
card
cash
check

child
clothing
command
diet
disease
drugs
drugstore
examination
gown
grain
health history / histories
height
insurance
jewelry
laboratory / laboratories
minute
payment plan
pharmacy
physical exam
prescription

protein
receptionist
robe
smoking
symptom
table
telephone
temperature
visit
vitamins
waiting room

Object Pronouns

her
him
it
me
them
us
you

Verbs

arrive
bill
check
come
complete
fill
give
may
put on
return
sign
sit
smoke
stand
take off
wait

Expressions

feel nauseated
make sure

 If you want to review vocabulary and complete additional activities related to this unit, go to the Read to Succeed 1 Web site at http://esl.college.hmco.com/students

CHAPTER 7

There Are Problems in My House

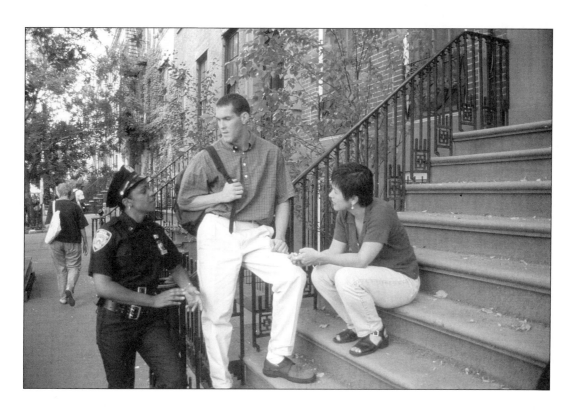

Reading 1   Family Problems

Before You Read

▶**EXERCISE 1** **Look at the pictures below. Then discuss these questions with a partner or a small group.**

1. What are the problems in this family?

2. Is there a similar problem in your community? How do you know?

3. Are alcohol and drugs problems in other countries? Explain.

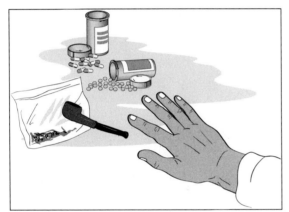

A.

B.

C.

D.

E.

▶**EXERCISE 2** **Listen to your teacher read each sentence. Say the sentences after your teacher. Then match each sentence with the correct picture.**

1. My mom is frequently crying. _____

2. He is often mad at us. _____

3. My sister and I are always crying, too. _____

4. He is hitting my mom more. _____

5. I see him using drugs now. _____

▶**EXERCISE 3** **Answer these questions.**

1. A person who drinks too much alcohol is an _____.

2. A person who is addicted to illegal drugs is a _____.

3. A counselor _____ people with problems.

4. What do you think the problems are in this family? _____

   _____

5. What is the title of the reading? _____

   _____

6. What is the main idea? Read the <u>underlined</u> sentence. Write it here:

   _____

7. Is alcoholism a problem in your native country? _____

   _____

8. What is a drug addict addicted to? _____

   _____

9. Do people visit drug and alcohol counselors in your native country? _____

   _____

10. Physical abuse is _____.
    a. hitting   b. liking   c. drugs

Words from the Reading*

career	problem
counselor	smoke
hit	

*Your teacher can help you understand these words and others listed at the end of the chapter and on the Web site at http://esl.college.hmco.com/students

Read to find out about this family's problems.

Family Problems

We are having bad family problems in our house right now. My parents are not happy. My name is John, and I am ten years old. My sister, Sharon, is seven. Mom says we are having dangerous problems. Sharon and I think it is our **fault.** My mother says our dad is drinking more and more. He frequently smokes marijuana. He sometimes uses cocaine. Things are really bad.

My dad sometimes hits my mom when he is drunk on alcohol or high on drugs. Sharon and I always cry when he gets mad. He often calls in sick to work. My dad **wastes** the family's money on alcohol and drugs. Mom says there is seldom money for food and rent. He is always mad, and we are afraid of him. I want to leave home and never come back. I don't want him to hit Mom anymore. Mom says we have to leave the house. It is dangerous for us at home.

Mom thinks a family counselor is a good idea. She says it is good for the family to talk about problems with a counselor. She wants to make an appointment for my dad at a drug abuse clinic and at an alcohol program. My mom is calling today. She wants the family to be strong. She is also talking to a career counselor. The counselor wants her to have career **training** and a job. I want my family to be happy. My mom wants Sharon and me to **behave** and study hard in school.

behave	to act
fault	mistake or responsibility
training	instruction or education
waste	to spend uselessly or badly

 **Comprehension**

►**EXERCISE 4** **Write T (true) or F (false) for each statement.**

_____ 1. The problems in John's house are not serious.

_____ 2. John's sister's name is Sharon, and she is seven.

_____ 3. The family is having dangerous problems.

_____ 4. The family's problems are the children's fault.

_____ 5. The father is using drugs.

_____ 6. The mother is drinking alcohol every day.

_____ 7. The father is physically abusing the mother.

_____ 8. The family has a lot of money.

_____ 9. A counselor is a good idea for the family.

_____ 10. The mother wants training and a job.

►**EXERCISE 5** **Write the answer that completes the sentence.**

1. They are having bad _____.

2. The children think _____.

3. The _____ is drinking _____.

4. _____ are always crying.

5. The father wastes money on _____.

6. The mother thinks _____ is a good idea.

7. The mother wants to make _____ for the father.

8. The mother wants the children to _____.

▶**EXERCISE 6 Read the questions and answer them orally with your teacher. Then answer the questions orally with a classmate. At home, write the answers for homework. Answer in complete sentences.**

1. What is the name of the boy? _____

2. How old is this boy? _____

3. Does he have a sister? _____

4. Is the family happy or unhappy? _____

5. Who is using cocaine? _____

6. Who is hitting the mother? _____

7. Is Dad calling in sick to work? _____

8. Is there money for food and rent? _____

9. Who is always mad? _____

10. What does the mother say is a good idea? _____

11. What appointment does the mother want to make? _____

12. Is the mother talking to a career counselor? _____

    _____

13. Who wants a job? _____

    _____

14. Who wants the family to be strong? _____

    _____

▶**EXERCISE 7** **Circle the number of the main idea for each paragraph.**

Paragraph 1:

1. John is ten years old, and Sharon is seven.

2. The parents are not happy.

3. There are serious problems in the house.

Paragraph 2:

1. There is no money for food and rent.

2. There is physical abuse in the family.

3. John and Sharon are crying all the time.

Paragraph 3:

1. A job is a good idea.

2. Family counseling is a good idea.

3. The father does not talk to his children.

📖 Vocabulary Practice

▶**EXERCISE 8 Write the correct adverb of frequency to complete the sentence.**

Adverbs of Frequency

Adverbs of frequency answer the question *how often?*

100%	80%	70%	50%	5%	0%
always	frequently	often	sometimes	seldom	never

With *to be:*   *He is always on time.* (subject + to be + adverb)
With other verbs: *She always works hard.* (subject + adverb + verb)

1. Dad _____ smokes marijuana.

2. He _____ uses cocaine.

3. Sharon and I _____ cry.

4. Dad _____ calls in sick to work.

5. Mom says there is _____ money for food and rent.

6. I don't want any problems. I will _____ use drugs.

▶**EXERCISE 9 Write the correct synonym for the underlined word. A synonym is a word with the same or a similar meaning. Look for the word in paragraph (¶) 1, 2, or 3.**

1. We are having <u>difficulties</u> in our house. (¶1, line 1) _____*problems*_____

2. Mom says we are having <u>unsafe</u> problems. (¶1, line 3–4) _____

3. He is smoking <u>pot</u> frequently. (¶1, line 5–6) _____

4. Mom says Dad <u>beats</u> her. (¶2, line 1) _____

5. He often calls in <u>ill</u> to work. (¶2, line 3) _____

6. There is no money for family <u>necessities</u>. (¶2, line 4–5) _____
   _____ (two words)

7. Sharon and I are <u>scared</u> of him. (¶2, line 5) _____

8. A family <u>advisor</u> is a good idea. (¶3, line 1) _____

9. She wants the family to be <u>united</u>. (¶3, line 3) _____

10. I <u>desire for</u> my family to be strong. (¶3, line 4) _____

 Grammar Hints: Present Progressive

▶**EXERCISE 10** **Write the Present Progressive of the verb indicated.**

Present Progressive
The Present Progressive is formed with *to be* + verb + *-ing*.

I am looking for a career and a job now. (look)   *We are having problems at home.* (hav¢)
He is smoking a cigarette right now. (smok¢)   *Are you drinking too much alcohol?* (drink)
Dad is leaving home. (leav¢)   *They are talking to a counselor.* (talk)

1. He _____ in sick to work now. (call)

2. Dad _____ us more and more. (hit)

3. We _____ bad problems at home this week. (have)

4. My father _____ money on drugs. (waste)

5. I _____ too much Coca-Cola. I am full! (drink)

6. She _____ too many cigarettes tonight. (smoke)

7. John _____ home today. (leave)

8. We _____ in a large city now. (live)

9. _____ Mom _____ to a counselor this morning? (talk)

10. The children _____ very hard in school this semester. (study)

11. Dad _____ not _____ now. (work)

12. _____ you _____ milk or coffee? (drink)

13. Where _____ you _____ now? (live)

14. Mom _____ an application for a job today. (complete)

15. A counselor _____ my family with our problems this week. (help)

Reading 2   We Have to Leave

Before You Read

▶**EXERCISE 11** **Scan the reading below. Then answer these questions.**

1. A woman goes to a shelter when there are unsafe _____ at home.

2. A child _____ clinic is good for a child who is abused.

3. Sandra wants to take classes at the community _____.

4. What is the title of the reading? _____

5. What is a possible solution for the family? _____

_____

6. Do you think this is a common problem? Why or why not? _____

_____

Words from the Reading*

abuse	life
calm	relaxed
clinic	safe
education	

*Your teacher can help you understand these words and
others listed at the end of the chapter and on the Web
site at http://esl.college.hmco.com/students

Read to find out the solution for the family.

⌒ We Have to Leave

Sandra and the children are now living in a women's **shelter.** They are safe and relaxed. She and the children feel calm and happy now. Sandra says, "We aren't crying anymore." The children are now happy in school. They are studying and paying attention more. The children and their mom are now talking about their problems. Sandra calls her husband and asks, "Do you want help?" He doesn't listen to her, and he doesn't want help. Her husband still has serious problems with alcohol, drugs, and abuse. He is always out with his friends and doesn't go home.

Sandra now has help from a counselor, Mrs. Martinez. Sandra says a **solution** is possible. She is going to look for a job. She also wants to take classes for a career. Sandra is going to call the community college and a career counselor tomorrow about classes. She wants job training and an education. Sandra is calling a counselor for the children at the child abuse clinic. She talks to other women at the shelter. The children also have friends at the shelter. Sandra wants her husband to call Alcoholics Anonymous and the Drug Abuse Prevention Center. She wants a good life for her family. She also wants her husband to find a **solution** for his problems.

shelter	a safe place to go or live
solution	answer

Comprehension

▶**EXERCISE 12** **Write T (true) or F (false) for each statement.**

_____ 1. Sandra and the kids are still at home.

_____ 2. She and the children are happy and calm.

_____ 3. Her husband has no problems.

_____ 4. The family doesn't have problems.

_____ 5. The father is talking about his problems.

_____ 6. Sandra's husband is always home.

_____ 7. Sandra wants a divorce.

_____ 8. Mrs. Martinez is the father's counselor.

_____ 9. Sandra is calling a child abuse clinic.

_____ 10. Sandra needs help from Alcoholics Anonymous.

▶**EXERCISE 13** Circle the number of the main idea for each paragraph.

Paragraph 1:

1. They are crying all the time.

2. The mother and children are living in a shelter.

3. The father is never home.

Paragraph 2:

1. The mother doesn't want to be at home.

2. She doesn't have any money.

3. Sandra is now receiving help at the shelter.

▶**EXERCISE 14** Read the questions and answer them orally with your teacher. Then answer the questions orally with a classmate. At home, write the answers for homework. Answer in complete sentences.

Why questions:

1. Why do Sandra and the kids leave the house? *They leave because it is not safe at home.*

   _____

2. Why does the family have problems? _____

   _____

3. Why do you think the kids are doing better in school now? _____

   _____

4. Why is the father never home? _____

   _____

5. Why do you think Sandra is calling the child abuse clinic? _____

   _____

Other questions:

1. Who feels safe and relaxed? _____

_____

2. Does the father still have problems? _____

_____

3. How are the children at school? _____

_____

4. Who doesn't have a job? _____

_____

5. How many children do Sandra and her husband have? _____

_____

6. Who asks, "Do you want help?" _____

_____

7. Who doesn't listen? _____

_____

8. Are there other families at the shelter? _____

_____

9. What is a good service for alcoholics? _____

_____

10. Where does Sandra want to study? _____

_____

Vocabulary Practice

▶**EXERCISE 14** Write the correct synonym for the <u>underlined</u> word. A synonym is a word with the same or a similar meaning. Look for the word in paragraph (¶) 1 or 2.

1. Sandra and the children are living in a <u>safe house</u> (¶1, line 1) _____

2. Sandra and the children are <u>calm</u>. (¶1, line 2) _____

3. Her husband has <u>important</u> problems. (¶1, line 7) _____

4. Sandra still <u>phones</u> her husband. (¶1, line 5) _____

5. Sandra now has an <u>advisor</u>. (¶2, line 1) _____

6. They are looking for an <u>answer</u>. (¶2, line 1) _____

7. There are other <u>ladies</u> at the shelter. (¶2, line 4) _____

8. Sandra's <u>spouse</u> needs to call AA. (¶2, line 5) _____

Expansion Activities

▶**Activity 1   What Happens Next?**   *Write a conclusion to the story about Sandra and her children. Think about these questions:*

Where do they go after the shelter?

Does the father see a doctor about his problems?

Does Sandra take classes or get a job?

Does the family solve its problems?

Share your conclusion with the class.

▶ **Activity 2 Write and Present a Dialogue** *Choose one of the following situations to write a dialogue about with a partner. Practice the dialogue with your partner and present it to the class.*

A. A Friend in Need

Sandra has a friend, Maria. They met in a drug abuse rehab center, where they stopped taking drugs and talked to counselors. Sandra and Maria are home now, and they like to share their feelings and ideas. Write a dialogue between Maria and Sandra.

B. The Next Generation

John is ten years old. He knows a boy, Sam, who is thirteen years old. Sam offers John some alcohol. What does John do? Write a dialogue between John and Sam.

Vocabulary List

Adjectives

afraid

alcoholic

better

calm

common

dangerous

drunk

high

mad

more

relaxed

safe

sick

Possessive Adjectives

her

his

its

my

our

their

your

Adverbs

frequently

never

physically

really

seldom

sometimes

still

Nouns

abuse

clinic

cocaine

community / communities

dad

fault

house

marijuana

mom

money

necessity / necessities

pot

problem

shelter

thing

work

Community Services

Alcoholics Anonymous

child abuse clinic

drug abuse clinic

drug rehab center

women's shelter

Object Pronouns

her

him

it

me

them

us

you

Verbs

abuse

beat

behave

cry / cries

do / does

drink

has / have

hit

leave

phone

use

If you want to review vocabulary and complete additional activities related to this unit, go to the Read to Succeed 1 Web site at http://esl.college.hmco.com/students

CHAPTER 8

Dating and Holidays in the United States

Reading 1   I Want to Date Her

Before You Read

▶**EXERCISE 1** **Discuss these questions with a partner or a small group.**

1. Is there dating in your culture?

2. What is an appropriate place to take a person on a date? Circle your answer.

   A. Out to dinner?   Yes   No

   B. Bicycling?   Yes   No

   C. Dancing at a discotheque?   Yes   No

3. What other places are acceptable for dates?

4. Do you go out with an American? If so, where do you go?

5. Are your date's customs different? How?

▶**EXERCISE 2** **Complete the sentences.**

1. A synonym for <u>date</u> is _____ with.

2. A synonym for <u>female</u> is a _____ .

3. A <u>male</u> is the same as a _____ .

Words from the Reading*

confused	funny	male	people
date	go out	meet	person
female	invite	parents	

*Your teacher can help you understand these words and
others listed at the end of the chapter and on the Web site
at http://esl.college.hmco.com/students

▶**EXERCISE 3** **Scan (read quickly) the first and last sentence of each
paragraph in the reading below, then answer the questions.**

Paragraph 1: Who does Juan want to date? _____

Paragraph 2: Who is telling him about single people? _____

Paragraph 3: What doesn't Juan know? _____

Read to find out about American dating customs.

∩ I Want to Date Her

Juan García is from Guatemala. He wants to go out with Susan, an American girl. Juan talks to her at work and at school. She is friendly, intelligent, and funny. Susan has many male and female friends. Juan sees many different and new **customs** in the United States. He doesn't understand the words *boyfriend, girlfriend,* and *friend.* He says, "I'm confused about American **customs** and about where to invite Susan!"

Juan's American friends are telling him about Americans and **dating.** They say that some people date one person and other people date two people at the same time. Other people go out with only one person for a while but are not **engaged.** Sometimes a single person lives in an apartment separate from the family. Sometimes young women invite friends to their apartment for lunch. At times, a woman invites a man to dinner and pays! Some women think they have to be careful on dates.

Juan's friends tell him that there are different **customs** here. His friends also say that not all single Americans are the same.

Juan doesn't know where to take Susan. He is thinking about first taking her home to meet his parents for a family New Year's party. His friends say that it is too soon. They tell Juan that good places to take her are the movies, dinner, jogging, a play, a party, dancing, or a concert. Now Juan wants to take Susan someplace fun—maybe dancing!

customs	traditions
dating	going out with someone
engaged	promised to be married

Comprehension

▶**EXERCISE 4** **Read the sentence, then place a check in the correct column.**

	True	False	Not enough information to know
1. Juan is thinking about asking Susan for a date.	✓		
2. Susan is single.			
3. Juan is a busy person.			
4. Juan has American friends.			
5. All single Americans live in apartments separate from their parents.			
6. Susan wants to go dancing with Juan.			
7. Sometimes a woman invites a man to dinner and pays.			

▶**EXERCISE 5** Circle the number of the main idea for each paragraph.

Paragraph 1:

1. Juan is a student.

2. Juan is friendly.

3. Juan wants to date Susan.

Paragraph 2:

1. All single people are not the same.

2. Juan is confused.

3. Juan lives with his parents.

Paragraph 3:

1. Juan's parents want to meet Susan.

2. There are many places to take Susan.

3. Susan doesn't want to go out with Juan.

▶**EXERCISE 6** Read the questions and answer them orally with your teacher. Then answer the questions orally with a classmate. At home, write the answers for homework. Answer in complete sentences.

About the reading:

1. What does Juan want? _____

_____

2. Is Susan Brazilian or American? _____

_____

3. Does Susan have a nice personality? How do you know? _____

_____

4. What is Juan confused about? _____

_____

5. How many people do Americans go out with? _____

_____

6. Where do some American women invite a man to dinner? _____

_____

7. Where is Juan taking Susan? _____

_____

Why questions:

1. Why does Juan want to date Susan? *He wants to date Susan because she is friendly, intelligent, and funny.*

2. Why is he confused about customs? _____

3. Why are American friends telling him about single people in the United States?

4. Why do friends tell Juan not to take Susan home to meet his parents? _____

About you and your culture:

1. What is a date? _____

2. What do you think about dating American people? _____

3. Who pays for a date in your culture? _____

4. Where do single people live in your native country? _____

5. What is your opinion about single women inviting men to their apartment for lunch?

6. What are some rules about dating in your culture? _____

7. Where is an appropriate place to take a person on a date? _____

8. How are American young people the same or different from young people in other countries? _____

9. Is there dating in your culture? Describe it. _____

Vocabulary Practice

►**EXERCISE 7** **Scan the reading and look for the synonyms for the underlined words.**

1. Juan wants to <u>date</u> Susan. (¶1, line 1) _____*go out with*_____

2. She is friendly, <u>smart</u>, and cute. (¶1, line 3) _____

3. He says, "I am <u>unclear</u> about the customs." (¶1, line 5–6) _____

4. They are telling him about <u>unmarried</u> people. (¶2, line 4) _____

5. Some Americans date <u>a couple</u> of people. (¶2, line 2) _____

6. At times, a woman <u>asks</u> a man out. (¶2, line 6) _____

7. The <u>traditions</u> here are different. (¶2, line 7) _____

8. He is taking her to meet <u>his mom and dad</u>. (¶3, line 1–2) _____

9. I think <u>running</u> is good exercise. (¶3, line 3) _____

Reading 2   Why Do Americans Wear Green on March 17?

Before You Read

►**EXERCISE 8** **Complete the sentences.**

1. I _____ New Year's with my family.

2. Going to the movies with friends is _____.

3. A short funny story is a _____.

Words from the Reading*

celebrate   costumes   holiday

*Your teacher can help you understand these words and others listed at the end of the chapter and on the Web site at http://esl.college.hmco.com/students

---

▶**EXERCISE 9** **Scan (read quickly) the first and last sentence of each paragraph in the reading below, then answer the questions.**

1. What is the title of the reading? _____

_____

2. What holidays do Americans celebrate? _____

_____

3. What holidays are the same in your country? _____

_____

Read to find out about American holidays.

Why Do Americans Wear Green on March 17?

St. Patrick's Day and Halloween are holidays that are not celebrated in many countries. Do you celebrate St. Patrick's Day in March by wearing green or drinking green beer? Does your American friend tell you a lie on April 1? Do you see people on the street with scary or funny masks and costumes on October 31? Are these American holiday customs very different for you? Americans celebrate several important holidays. Some holidays are **religious** or cultural, and some holidays are for fun. Others are **national** holidays, and many people do not work.

Here are some American holidays and celebrations:

New Year's Day (January 1)
Americans celebrate with family or friends at home with a **meal.** Some people watch football games on television. On New Year's Eve (December 31), people have a special dinner or party. Some homeless shelters serve a free **meal.**

Valentine's Day (February 14)
Men and women give **gifts,** flowers, or candy. Young children in school give friends a Valentine's card. Red and white are popular colors for Valentine's Day.

Presidents' Day (third Monday of February)

This day in February is a **national** holiday. We celebrate both President Washington's and President Lincoln's birthdays.

St. Patrick's Day (March 17)

On this day, many people wear green. Some restaurants and bars have green decorations and green beer. Everyone is Irish on this fun day. Children sometimes pinch friends who do not wear green.

April Fool's Day (April 1)

People tell you lies or jokes for fun on this day.

Easter and Passover (early spring) / Spring Break (a week in March or April)

On Easter, a **religious** holiday that is also for fun, children color hard-boiled eggs. Adults hide the eggs for the children to find. Some children get an Easter basket with rabbit-shaped candies. Some Jewish people have a traditional dinner (Seder) during Passover. For spring break, students in public schools as well as in colleges and universities get one week of vacation from school.

Mother's Day (second Sunday of May)

People take their mother out to eat or give her flowers or chocolates. Some husbands make the **meals** on this special Sunday.

Memorial Day (last Monday of May)

Americans think about family, friends, and soldiers who died in wars. On this **national** holiday, many people don't work. Some people hang an American flag in front of their house.

Father's Day (third Sunday of June)

Fathers receive a card or a **gift.**

Fourth of July (Independence Day)

This holiday celebrates the day the United States won its freedom from England. Most Americans do not work on this **national** holiday. People have barbecues or picnics. There are usually local parades and fireworks. Red, white, and blue—the colors of the American flag—are special colors for July 4th.

Labor Day (first Monday of September)

On this **national** holiday, the American worker is important. People don't work. They have picnics on the beach or barbeques at home. It is the end of summer vacation.

Ramadan (October)

Ramadan is the ninth month of the Islamic calendar, but it is not always the same month. It is a **religious** month, and Muslims fast during the daylight hours for a whole month. People also purify their bodies and minds during this time.

Halloween (October 31)

Children wear costumes and scary or funny masks. The children go trick-or-treating at night—they knock on doors and ask for candy. Halloween is a day of fun. Adults often have costume parties. Orange and black are popular colors for Halloween.

Thanksgiving (last Thursday of November)

Families have a traditional **meal** that usually includes stuffed turkey, cranberry sauce, and pumpkin pie.

Homeless people have a special meal at a shelter or a church. Some people watch a football game on television. Most Americans do not work on this **national** holiday.

Christmas and Hanukkah (December)

These are **religious** and cultural holidays. Families give **gifts** and have a special **meal.** Some families have a Christmas tree or a menorah. Green and red are important Christmas colors, and Santa Claus visits the stores to see the children. During Hanukkah, some children play with a toy called a dreidel.

gift	a present for someone
meal	breakfast, lunch, or dinner
national	all of the country
religious	about God

Comprehension

►EXERCISE 10 Write T (true) or F (false) for each statement.

_____ 1. All American holidays are religious.

_____ 2. Some American holidays are for fun.

_____ 3. People wear green on New Year's.

_____ 4. People give candy on Valentine's Day.

_____ 5. Some people give baskets on St. Patrick's Day.

_____ 6. Some children color eggs for Easter.

_____ 7. On Memorial Day, people think about soldiers who have died in wars.

_____ 8. The Fourth of July is Father's Day.

_____ 9. For Halloween, people wear costumes and masks.

_____ 10. Americans give gifts on Thanksgiving.

►**EXERCISE 11   Write the letter of the phrase that completes the sentence.**

1. For Christmas _____   a. Americans eat stuffed turkey.

2. For New Year's _____   b. people take their mother out.

3. For Thanksgiving _____   c. Americans tell jokes or lies.

4. For Valentine's Day _____   d. people celebrate American independence.

5. On Halloween _____   e. some people have a decorated tree.

6. On St. Patrick's Day _j_____   f. people have special food and watch television.

7. On Labor Day _____   g. children give friends special cards.

8. For April Fool's Day _____   h. children go trick-or-treating.

9. On the Fourth of July _____ i. the American worker is important.

10. For Mother's Day _____   j. everyone is Irish.

►**EXERCISE 12   Read the questions and answer them orally with your teacher. Then answer the questions orally with a classmate. At home, write the answers for homework. Answer in complete sentences.**

About the reading:

1. On what holiday do Americans pinch their friends? _____

   _____

2. On what holiday do people tell stories or play jokes? _____

   _____

3. When do Americans think about soldiers who have died in wars? _____

   _____

4. Name two holidays when homeless people get a meal? _____

   _____

5. On what special day do Americans give dads a gift? _____

   _____

About your culture:

1. What holidays in your native country are the same as American holidays? _____

_____

2. Is there a day when you remember dead family members in your culture? When?

_____

3. Do you have an independence day in your country? Tell about it. _____

_____

4. How do people celebrate Easter in your culture? Is Easter religious or fun in your

culture? _____

_____

5. How is Valentine's or Friendship Day celebrated in your native country? _____

_____

Vocabulary Practice

▶**EXERCISE 13 Complete each sentence with a word from the box.**

barbecues	independence	jokes	national	religious	scary

1. People wear _____ masks for Halloween.

2. People have _____ on the beach for Labor Day.

3. Memorial Day is a _____ holiday in the United States.

4. Friends tell _____ and lies for April Fool's Day.

5. Americans celebrate their _____ on July 4th.

6. Christmas is a _____ holiday and also fun.

►**EXERCISE 14** **Read the sentence. Then circle the synonym, or word with the same meaning as the <u>underlined</u> word.**

1. Juan wants to <u>go out</u> with Susan.   a. date   b. watch   c. hide

2. A disco is an <u>acceptable</u> place
   to take her.   a. dangerous   b. confused c. appropriate

3. Halloween is a day of <u>excitement</u>
   for children.   a. school   b. fun   c. cards

4. I always <u>see</u> that television program.   a. listen   b. enjoy   c. watch

5. She is very <u>nice</u> to people at the
   restaurant.   a. friendly   b. serious   c. crazy

►**EXERCISE 15** **Change the word by adding the suffix indicated. Use your dictionary to check the spelling.**

A **suffix** is a syllable at the end of a word that changes the meaning.
-ous: advantage / advantage<u>ous</u>
-al: nature / natur**al**
-ly: slow / slow**ly**

---

1. **-ous:** cavern _____   danger *dangerous*   humor _____

   mountain _____   nausea _____   religion _____

   rigor _____   scandal _____   vigor _____

2. **-al:** continent _____   culture _____   education _____

   historic _____   intern _____   nation _____

   origin _____   recreation _____   tradition _____

3. **-ly:** careful _____   cheap _____   different _____

   friend _____   honest _____   kind _____

   loud _____   nice _____   safe _____

   separate _____   total _____

Grammar Hints: More practice with Object Pronouns

▶**EXERCISE 16** **Read each sentence. Change the <u>underlined</u> word or words from a noun or nouns to an object pronoun.**

Singular:	me	you	him	her	it
Plural:	us	you	them		

1. Paul takes his <u>mother</u> out on Mother's Day.

   Paul takes ____*her*____ out on Mother's Day.

2. Some people have <u>barbeques</u> on the beach.

   Some people have _____ on the beach.

3. His friends tell <u>Juan</u> about dating customs.

   His friends tell _____ about dating customs.

4. They tell <u>Juan and me</u> about American single people.

   They tell _____ about American single people.

5. <u>Susan</u> wants to go out with Juan.

   She hopes he invites _____ to dinner.

6. I am inviting <u>you and your</u> husband to dinner.

   I am inviting _____ to dinner.

7. Do you like <u>pizza</u>?

   Yes, I like _____ with pepperoni.

8. I am celebrating New Year's with <u>Maria</u>.

   I like to celebrate with _____.

Expansion Activities

► **Activity 1 Write a Valentine Note** *Juan is at a card shop. He wants to send a Valentine card to Sandra. Help him choose the Valentine card with the best message. Discuss with a partner which card is the best for Juan. Then write a note on the card from Juan to Susan.*

► **Activity 2 Make That Call!** *Susan calls Juan to ask him out on a date. Does he say yes? Where do they want to go? What transportation do they use? What day and at what time do they go? With a partner, write the dialogue for this phone call. Practice the dialogue and present it to the class or a group.*

Vocabulary List

Adjectives

acceptable
appropriate
confused
crazy
cute
dead
engaged
female
free
green
homeless
Irish
male
national
others
public
red
religious
scary
several
stuffed
traditional

Adverb

soon

Nouns

bar
barbecue
basket
beer
bicycling
boyfriend
candy / candies
card
chocolate
color
concert
costume
cranberry sauce
culture
custom
dancing
dating
dinner

egg
firework
flag
flower
football
fun
game
gift
girl
hiking
holiday
independence
jogging
joke
lady / ladies
lie
lunch
mask
meals
movie
parade
party / parties

picnic
play
pumpkin pie
rule
soldier
tradition
vacation
while

Holidays

April Fool's Day
Christmas
Easter
Father's Day
Fourth of July
Halloween
Hanukkah
Labor Day
Memorial Day
Mother's Day
Passover
Ramadan
St. Patrick's Day
Seder

Thanksgiving
Valentine's Day

Prepositions

about
in front of

Verbs

celebrate
color
date
describe
go out
invite
meet
pay
pinch
remember
wear

If you want to review vocabulary and complete additional activities related to this unit, go to the Read to Succeed 1 Web site at http://esl.college.hmco.com/students

Careers, Counseling, and Community

Job Bank

Counseling Service

African-American Community Service Center

CHAPTER 9

Looking for a Job

Reading 1   A Layoff

Before You Read

▶ **EXERCISE 1   Discuss these questions with a partner or a small group.**

1. What kinds of jobs do you look for?

2. What are some different ways to look for a job?

3. When you look for a job, what is important?

▶**EXERCISE 2** **Listen to your teacher read each sentence. Say the sentences after your teacher. Then match each sentence with the correct picture.**

A.

B.

C.

D.

E.

F.

1. She is completing an application. _____

2. A medical exam is necessary. _____

3. He has experience as a farmworker, a mechanic, a construction worker, and assembler. _____

4. They are having another child. _____

5. Smith Electronics is laying off 200 workers. _____

6. He is looking for a job in the classified ads. _____

▶**EXERCISE 3** **Read the statements and circle agree or disagree.**

1. A synonym for **go to** school is **attend** school.   agree   disagree

2. A synonym for **finish** school is **complete** school.   agree   disagree

3. When you are **worried,** you are **calm.**   agree   disagree

Words from the Reading*

attend	look
complete	optimistic
finish	

*Your teacher can help you understand these words and others listed at the end of the chapter and on the Web site at http://esl.college.hmco.com/students

▶**EXERCISE 4** **Scan the reading below. Then answer these questions.**

1. Where does José work? What does he do there? _____

_____

2. What is the problem at his job? _____

_____

3. Where is José looking for a job? _____

_____

Read to find out why José is applying for a new job.

∩ A Layoff

José and Olivia Lopez work very hard. José is working and studying full-time. José is studying ESL and electronics at a city college during the day. He is an electronics assembler at Smith Electronics at night. Olivia is a homemaker, and she works very **hard.** She wants to attend a city college when José finishes his program. José is looking for another job because they are having a second child in three months.

José is very **worried** about his **job** at Smith Electronics. There is not enough work. Smith Electronics is going to **lay off** 200 workers. José needs another **job.** José has very good skills. In the United States, José has **experience** as a farmworker and a mechanic. He also has five years of **experience** as an assembler, and he is never late.

José is looking for a **job** in different places. First, he is looking at the employment office and at a **job** agency. Next, he is reading the want ads in the classified section of the newspaper. Apple Electronics is looking for an electronics assembly supervisor. José says to Olivia, "I am applying for that **job!** The pay is good, the medical benefits are excellent, and I have experience. I need to fill out an application and get a medical exam. Then they want an interview." José is optimistic. He says, "I'm completing an application today!"

experience	years of work
hard	difficult
job	position at work
lay off	stop working temporarily
worried	concerned

 Comprehension

▶**EXERCISE 5** **Write T (true) or F (false) for each statement.**

_____ 1. José is working part-time.

_____ 2. He is a full-time student in high school.

_____ 3. José is a single man.

_____ 4. Olivia is a homemaker.

_____ 5. José does not need to study English.

_____ 6. José has a lot of experience.

_____ 7. They are having a second child.

_____ 8. José is reading the want ads in the newspaper.

_____ 9. He is applying for a job at Smith Electronics.

_____ 10. An application, medical exam, and interview are necessary.

_____ 11. José is an electronics assembler at Apple Electronics.

_____ 12. A housewife is the same as a homemaker.

_____ 13. Smith Electronics is laying José off because he is not a good worker.

_____ 14. José has good skills but not much experience.

_____ 15. José is looking for a job by asking his friends and family.

_____ 16. José's wife, Olivia, is not interested in an education.

▶**EXERCISE 6** **Circle the number of the main idea for each paragraph.**

Paragraph 1:

1. Olivia is a homemaker.

2. José and Olivia work hard in the United States.

3. ESL is very interesting.

Paragraph 2:

1. José has experience, and he wants a new job.

2. José is never late.

3. José has experience as a farmworker.

Paragraph 3:

1. The employment office is on State Street.

2. José is reading the newspaper.

3. José is looking in different places and is applying for a new job.

▶**EXERCISE 7** **Read the questions and answer them orally with your teacher. Then answer the questions orally with a classmate. At home, write the answers for homework. Answer in complete sentences.**

1. What are the names of the wife and husband? _____

_____

2. Where is the wife working? _____

_____

3. Is José a day or night student? Is he studying full-time or part-time? _____

_____

4. Does José have experience in electronics assembly? _____

_____

5. Where is a good place to look for a job? _____

_____

6. What company is looking for a supervisor? _____

_____

7. Where is José applying for the new job? _____

_____

8. How is the pay at the new job? _____

_____

9. Is an interview necessary for the new job? _____

_____

Why questions:

1. Why do you think José is studying ESL? *José is studying ESL because English is not his first language.*

2. Why do you think José is an excellent worker? _____

_____

3. Why is he looking for another job? _____

_____

4. Why is he applying for an electronics assembly job? _____

_____

5. Why is he reading the classified section? _____

_____

Vocabulary Practice

▶**EXERCISE 8** **Read the sentence, then circle the letter of the correct answer.**

1. What is José Lopez studying at City College?

   a. business   b. assembly   c. ESL and electronics

2. What is he looking for?

   a. a job   b. a wife   c. a medical plan

3. What is José's job now?

   a. mechanic   b. assembler   c. farmworker

4. What is the problem at Smith Electronics?

   a. laying off workers   b. hiring workers   c. experience

5. Where is José looking for a job?

   a. sports page   b. editorial page   c. classified pages

6. What is good about the new job?

   a. the layoffs   b. pay and benefits   c. the supervisor

▶**EXERCISE 9** **Complete each sentence with a word from the box.**

application	benefits	experience	hard worker	interview
job	medical exam	pay	supervisor	want ads

1. I have two years _____ as a busboy.

2. An _____ with the boss is necessary.

3. José is a _____ and is never late.

4. I have a _____ at the doctor's office today.

5. She is completing an _____ for the new job.

6. José is applying for the new _____.

7. I am reading the _____ in the newspaper.

8. The _____ at Apple Electronics is excellent. It is $15 an hour.

9. José wants the job of assembly _____.

10. The medical _____ at Apple Electronics are fantastic!

Reading Charts and Graphs

▶EXERCISE 10

A. Study the graph about available jobs.

Jobs with most openings yearly

■ Salespersons
■ Food workers
■ Cashiers
□ Waitresses
■ Nurses

Retail salespersons, 207,280; food preparers / servers / fast-food workers, 202,340; cashiers, 198,230; waiters / waitresses, 147,920; registered nurses, 100,390.

Source: Bureau of Labor Statistics, 2002

B. Answer the questions about the chart.

1. How many salespersons do stores need each year? _____

2. How many food workers are needed? _____

3. What jobs in these areas require a college degree? _____

4. Are you working in one of these occupations now? _____

Reading 2   The Interview

Before You Read

▶**EXERCISE 11   Read the statements and circle agree or disagree.**

1. **End** is a synonym for **beginning.**   agree   disagree

2. **Question** is the antonym for **answer.**   agree   disagree

3. **Supervisor** is the same as **boss.**   agree   disagree

---

Words from the Reading*

confident	interviewer	prepare	supervisor
end	personnel office	question	

*Your teacher can help you understand these words and others listed at the end of the chapter and on the Web site at http://esl.college.hmco.com/students

---

▶**EXERCISE 12   Scan the reading below. Then answer these questions.**

1. What is the title? _____

_____

2. What is José having today? _____

_____

3. What does José do to prepare for the interview? _____

_____

4. What does José ask about? _____

_____

Read to find out about José's interview.

The Interview

Today is José's important **interview** at Apple Electronics. José's old supervisor at Smith Electronics helps José. He asks José questions every day to prepare for the interview. José is prepared and confident. He also has experience in electronics assembly. He is ready for all the questions. José arrives at the personnel office early. He is wearing nice clothes.

It is now time for the **interview.** First, he is saying hello to the interviewers. Next, José shakes their hand. Then they ask José about his experience. José is telling them about his **qualifications** and education. He is answering their questions well. José is saying that he is an excellent worker. Next, he says that he is never late. Then José is saying that he has experience. He is looking at the interviewers. José is confident and relaxed.

Finally, it is the end of the **interview.** José asks some questions about the job. He is asking about the hours, **salary,** and medical **benefits.** He also asks about the promotions and the pension plan. The **interview** is finally over. José shakes hands with the interviewers. He says, "Thank you." He hopes he gets the job.

benefits	help with medical costs
interview	asking and answering questions
qualifications	experience and education
salary	pay

 Comprehension

▶**EXERCISE 13** **Write T (true) or F (false) for each statement.**

_____ 1. An interview is not important.

_____ 2. José arrives late.

_____ 3. He is wearing nice clothes.

_____ 4. José shakes hands with the interviewers.

_____ 5. José does not answer their questions well.

_____ 6. José says that he is an excellent worker.

_____ 7. Finally, he asks some questions about school.

▶**EXERCISE 14** **Circle the letter of the correct answer.**

1. How is José for the interview?

   a. prepared and confident   b. late   c. absent

2. What is José ready for?

   a. work   b. the interview   c. school

3. Where is the interview?

   a. cafeteria   b. personnel office   c. at home

4. What is José telling the interviewers about?

   a. his qualifications and experience   b. his baby   c. his clothes

5. Finally, what is José asking about?

   a. hours, salary, and benefits   b. vacations   c. breaks

▶**EXERCISE 15** **Read the questions and answer them orally with your teacher. Then answer the questions orally with a classmate. At home, write the answers for homework. Answer in complete sentences.**

During the interview:

1. Is José getting to his interview late? _____

   _____

2. What office is the interview in? _____

   _____

3. What kind of clothes is José wearing? _____

   _____

4. Who is José saying hello to? _____

   _____

5. What is he telling them about? _____

   _____

6. Is José answering their questions badly? _____

   _____

7. What kind of worker is José? _____

_____

8. Is José nervous and stressed? _____

_____

9. Who is José looking at during the interview? _____

_____

10. Who is José shaking hands with? _____

_____

▶**EXERCISE 16** **Number the sentences in the correct order or sequence.**

_____ 1. The interview is finally over.

_____ 2. José is preparing for the interview.

_____ 3. It is now time for the interview.

_____ 4. He is saying he is never late.

_____ 5. José is applying for the new job.

_____ 6. The interviewers are asking about his experience.

_____ 7. Smith Electronics is laying off 200 workers.

_____ 8. He is asking about hours, salary, and promotions.

_____ 9. He is reading the want ads.

___*1*___ 10. José is working at Smith Electronics.

Vocabulary Practice

▶**EXERCISE 17** **Complete each sentence with a present progressive verb from the box.**

am answering	am applying	are arriving	am attending	are asking
are finishing	are having	are interviewing	are saying	~~are wearing~~
is calming	is completing	is looking	is shaking	is worrying

During the interview:

1. The interviewers _____*are wearing*_____ nice clothes to the interview.

2. You _____ at the interview early, aren't you?

3. They _____ hello to José.

4. The interviewers _____ him questions.

5. I _____ their questions well.

6. José and Olivia _____ a child in three months.

7. José _____ at the interviewers in the eye.

8. He is saying hello and _____ hands with the interviewers.

9. "I _____ for the job at Apple," says José.

10. José _____ an application today!

11. We _____ our homework now, then we are giving it to the teacher.

12. The supervisors _____ my friend right now in the personnel office.

13. I _____ a very nice college this year near my apartment.

14. Susan _____ now about her three tests tomorrow, so she can't concentrate.

15. The little girl is crying, so her mother _____ her down.

▶**EXERCISE 18** **Complete each sentence with an adjective from the box.**

confident	hard	medical	new
pension	personnel	serious	well

1. José is a _____ worker.

2. The interview is in the _____ office.

3. The new job has excellent _____ benefits.

4. There is a _____ problem at Smith Electronics.

5. José is applying for the _____ job.

6. José is answering the interviewers' questions _____ .

7. José is prepared for and _____ about the interview.

8. Apple Electronics has a good _____ plan.

▶**EXERCISE 19** **Say each word after your teacher. Then scan (read quickly) the list and circle the words about jobs.**

work	pension plan	theater	supervisor
clothing	layoffs	interviewers	benefits
promotions	interview	picnics	hours
job	nice clothes	classroom	dinner
application	employment office	classified section	parties
dancing	personnel office	applying	pay
experience	shorts	questions	qualifications
medical exam	want ads		

Expansion Activities

▶**Activity 1 Choose a Job for Olivia** *José now has a job, and he and Olivia have two children. Olivia wants to look for a job. She doesn't have much experience and she only wants to work part-time, but her English is improving and she's a hard worker. Read the classified ads below. Then choose which job you think is good for Olivia and give a reason for your choice.*

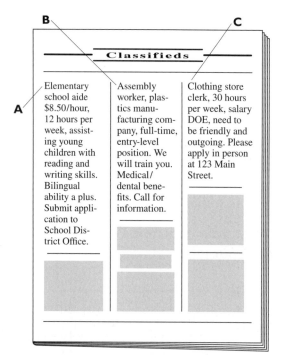

B

C

Classifieds

A

Elementary school aide $8.50/hour, 12 hours per week, assisting young children with reading and writing skills. Bilingual ability a plus. Submit application to School District Office.

Assembly worker, plastics manufacturing company, full-time, entry-level position. We will train you. Medical/dental benefits. Call for information.

Clothing store clerk, 30 hours per week, salary DOE, need to be friendly and outgoing. Please apply in person at 123 Main Street.

I think that the _____ job is good for

Olivia because _____

_____

_____

_____

▶**Activity 2 Time for an Interview!** *With a partner, prepare an interview between Olivia and the employer for one of the job ads in Activity 1. Write questions and answers. Then practice the interview with your partner and present the interview to your class.*

Here are some possible questions that you can use:

1. Do you have experience in this kind of work?

2. What are some good qualities that you have?

3. What do other supervisors or other people say about you?

4. What do you want to do in the future?

5. What do you do outside of work?

Vocabulary List

Adjectives

absent

confident

hard

optimistic

personnel

prepared

stressed

Adverbs

as

early

late

then

Nouns

agency / agencies

application

assembler

baby / babies

break

classified ad

clothes

construction worker

electronics assembly

employment office

end

hand

hello

hour

interview

interviewer

kind

layoff

occupation

personnel office

promotions

qualifications

salary / salaries

section

supervisor

Places to Look for Jobs

companies

family

friends

job agency

newspaper want ads

radio

school

television

Sections of Newspaper

classified pages

editorial page

sports page

Prepositions

at

during

for

in

to

Verbs

apply

finish / finishes

lay off

open

prepare

require

shake

start

tell

If you want to review vocabulary and complete additional activities related to this unit, go to the Read to Succeed 1 Web site at http://esl.college.hmco.com/students

CHAPTER 10

What Careers Should I Think About?

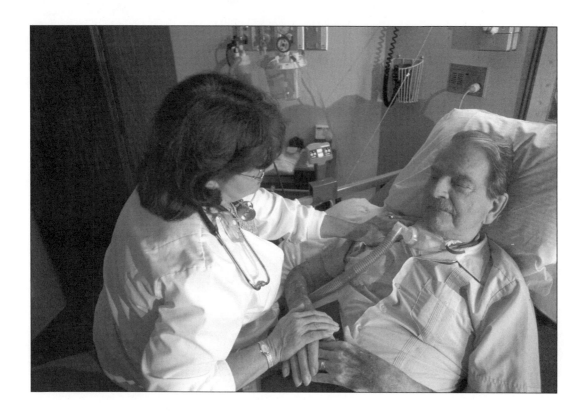

Reading 1 Careers and Money

Before You Read

▶**EXERCISE 1** Discuss these questions with a partner or a small group.

1. Are you going to want on-the-job training or a study program?

2. How long are you going to study?

3. What careers are you interested in?

►**EXERCISE 2** **Look at the pictures and statistics, and read the information. Then answer the questions.**

A. Workers needed in 2010 in four of the 25 fastest growing occupations and the pay in those occupations now.*

Computer Software Engineer, $67,700/yr.
760,100 more needed in 2010

Personal and Home Care Aide, $15,600/yr.
672,100 more needed in 2010

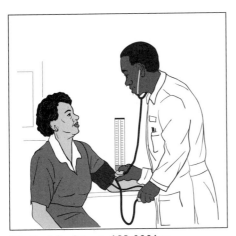

Medical Assistant, $23,000/yr.
515,800 more needed in 2010

Aerobics Instructor, $22,800/yr.
222,200 more needed in 2010

1. What career pays a very good salary? _____

2. What job is going to need about 500,000 workers in 2010? _____

3. What occupation earns a very low salary? _____

4. How many more aerobics teachers are we going to need in 2010?

_____

*Bureau of Labor Statistics, Office of Employment Projections, 2003.

B. Workers needed in 2010 in four of the top 25 occupations requiring an associate degree or a training program and the pay in those occupations now.

Computer Support Specialist, $36,500/yr.
995,900 needed in 2010

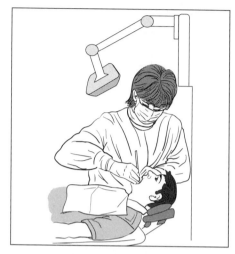

Dental Hygienist, $51,300/yr.
201,000 needed in 2010

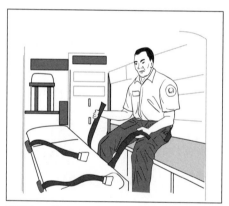

EMT or Paramedic, $22,500/yr.
226,000 needed in 2010

Registered Nurse (RN), $44,800/yr.
2,750,000 million needed in 2010

1. Which occupation is going to need almost a million workers in 2010?

   _____

2. Which careers earn more than a nurse? _____

3. Who makes less, a paramedic or a nurse? _____

4. What person works at a dental office? _____

▶**EXERCISE 3** **What do you think? Write T (true) or F (false) for each statement.**

_____ 1. A high school dropout makes more money than a community college graduate.

_____ 2. All new and popular jobs pay a lot of money.

_____ 3. A high school dropout earns a high salary later.

_____ 4. Short study programs pay more money later.

Words from the Reading*

fast-growing

opening

*Your teacher can help you understand these words and others listed at the end of the chapter and on the Web site at http://esl.college.hmco.com/students

---

▶**EXERCISE 4** **Scan (read quickly) the reading below, then answer the questions.**

1. Do you think a high school graduate makes more money than a high school dropout? (¶1)

   _____

2. Do occupations that have many openings always pay more? (¶2)

   _____

3. What occupations are going to have many openings? (¶2)

   _____

4. What jobs are growing very fast? (¶3)

   _____

Read about some careers and their salaries.

 # Careers and Money

The more education you have, the more money you make. A high school graduate earns about $1.2 million from twenty-five to sixty-five years of age.* A graduate from a community college with an associate **degree** makes more money than a high school graduate. If you complete a bachelor's **degree** at a university, you are going to earn about $2.1 million in your lifetime!*

Some occupations have many job openings, but the pay is sometimes low. There are many jobs at restaurants, stores, schools, and small businesses. How much money you make depends on the job. Nurses, teachers, and sales representatives make more money than medical assistants or aerobic teachers. For example, a nurse makes an **average** of $44,800[†] per year. Pay is lower for gardeners, restaurant workers, and salespersons. A waiter or waitress earns an **average** of $13,400[†] per year.

Some fast-growing careers do not pay a lot of money.[†] These occupations are in business, computers, health, and exercise. Some of these jobs require no study program. Others require four years of school. A home health aide takes care of sick people in their homes and earns $15,600 per year.[†] A computer support specialist makes $36,500.[†] Careers in medicine, business, law, science, and computers pay more money. They require a university **degree.** A petroleum engineer makes an **average** of $78,900[†] per year. A doctor who is an anesthesiologist earns an **average** of $145,600[†] per year.

When you think about a career, think about three things: how long you are going to study or train; how many jobs there are going to be in the future; and how much money you are likely to make. What is important is that the more you study, the more you are going to earn in the future.

average	typical amount
degree	a college or university diploma

*United States Census Bureau, 2002 estimates.

[†]United States Bureau of Labor Statistics, 2002 estimates.

 **Comprehension**

▶EXERCISE 5 **Circle the correct answer. Scan the reading again if necessary.**

A. Paragraph 1: The U.S. Census Bureau says that, if you finish high school,

1. you are going to earn $2.1 million during your life.

2. you are going to make $1.2 million during your life.

3. you are going to earn $1 million more than a college graduate.

B. Paragraph 2: There are many jobs in some occupations, but

1. the salary is very high.

2. the salary is the same as in other jobs.

3. the salary is sometimes not high.

C. Paragraph 3: The professions that pay a lot of money are in

1. home health care.

2. computers, science, law, business, and medicine.

3. aerobics teaching.

D. Paragraph 4: The three things to think about for a career are

1. vacations and promotions.

2. years of study, the number of jobs, and how much money.

3. supervisors and promotions.

▶**EXERCISE 6** **Read the questions and answer them orally with your teacher. Then answer the questions orally with a classmate. At home, write the answers for homework. Answer in complete sentences.**

Paragraph 1:

1. How much money is a high school graduate going to make in his or her lifetime?

   _____

2. How much more money does a community college graduate earn more than a high school graduate? _____

   _____

3. How much more money does a university graduate make than a high school graduate? _____

   _____

4. What salary does a university graduate make in his or her lifetime? _____

   _____

5. What does the paragraph say about education and salary? _____

   _____

Paragraph 2:

1. Do restaurant workers make a lot of money? _____

   _____

2. How much money does a waiter earn? Is that a high salary or a low salary?

   _____

3. Are there a lot of job openings at stores and restaurants? _____

   _____

Paragraph 3:

1. Which is a fast-growing occupation that is interesting for you? _____

   _____

2. Does a home health aide earn a lot of or a little money? _____

   _____

3. Which careers pay the most and the least money? _____

_____

4. How much money does an anesthesiologist make per year? _____

_____

5. Who earns about $80,000 per year? _____

_____

Paragraph 4:

1. What three things should you think about for a future career? _____

_____

Vocabulary Practice

▶EXERCISE 7 Complete the sentences.

1. There are _____ that are fast growing.

2. Some careers pay a lot of _____.

3. Two fast-growing occupations are _____ and _____.

4. A _____ takes care of sick people in their homes.

5. One career that pays a lot of money is _____.

6. The careers that pay the most require a _____ degree.

▶EXERCISE 8 Write a synonym for each word.

1. occupation   _____

2. in the coming years   _____

3. salary   _____

4. earn   _____

5. statistics   _____

Grammar Hints: *Be* + *going to* + infinitive for the future

▶**EXERCISE 9** Study the following information and examples.

To express the future: *be* + *going* + *infinitive verb*
She <u>is going to look</u> for a job.
I <u>am going to learn</u> English well.
We <u>are going to train</u> for a job.

A. Write an *infinitive* (to take, to have, to attend, to earn)

1. If I study for an associate degree, I am going _____ more money.

2. If she learns English well, she is going _____ a very good job.

3. We are going _____ a community college next year.

4. He is going _____ care of sick people in their homes.

5. My family is going _____ a short vacation next summer.

6. I am going _____ a lot of homework when I study nursing.

B. Write *be* (I am, you are, he is, we are, you are (pl.), they are) + *going to* (am going, is going, are going)

1. They _____ to study computers at the community college.

2. I _____ to earn a university degree later.

3. My sister _____ to transfer to the university after community college.

4. My brother _____ to earn $36,500 as a computer support specialist.

5. My sister and I _____ to leave home to attend a university

6. My class _____ to have to take a long difficult test next week.

Reading Charts and Graphs

▶EXERCISE 10

A. Study the chart and statistics about fast-growing jobs.

Four fast-growing jobs requiring a BA degree or higher (among top 25)

Occupation by Rank	Workers Needed 2000	Workers Needed 2010	% Change	Median Pay in 2000
1. Computer software engineer	380,000	760,100	100% more	$67,700
12. Social worker	83,100	115,700	39% more	$30,200
13. Elementary school teacher	234,000	320,100	37% more	$40,900
24. Veterinarian	58,600	77,300	32% more	$60,900

Source: Bureau of Labor Statistics

B. Answer the questions about the chart.

1. What degree do these jobs require? _____

2. Which career will need one hundred percent more workers in 2010?

   _____

3. Which occupation has the fewest workers? _____

4. What career is going to need 320,100 workers in 2010? _____

5. These people earn about thirty thousand dollars per year. _____

6. The United States is going to need thirty-nine percent more of these workers in
   2010. _____

7. The salary for these workers is almost $70,000. _____

8. What school do all these workers have to attend? _____

Reading 2   Careers for the Future

Before You Read

▶**EXERCISE 11   Discuss these questions with a partner or a small group.**

1. What careers are you thinking about?

2. Do you want a short or a long study program to prepare for a career?

3. How much money are you going to need per month as an older adult?

▶**EXERCISE 12   Listen to your teacher read the careers in parts A, B, and C. Repeat the careers. Then read each sentence and write the name of the career it describes.**

A.

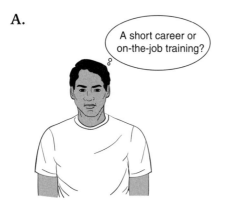

A short career or on-the-job training?

Dental assistant?   Hotel desk worker?

Home health aide?   Medical assistant?

1. This person works in a dental office. _____

2. He helps sick or elderly people in their homes. _____

3. She checks people in and out at a hotel. _____

4. This person works at a medical clinic or office. _____

B.

Computer support specialist?   Paramedic?

Dental hygienist?   Registered nurse?

1. She works with patients at a clinic or hospital. _____

2. He helps people with computer problems. _____

3. She drives an ambulance to medical emergencies. _____

4. This person cleans and polishes your teeth. _____

C.

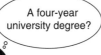

Computer software engineer?   Social worker?

School counselor?   Teacher?

1. This person helps students with problems. _____

2. This person assists families. _____

3. He designs computer programs. _____

4. She helps students learn and succeed at school. _____

►**EXERCISE 13 What do you think? Write T (true) or F (false) for each statement.**

_____ 1. A community college offers associate degrees.

_____ 2. A university offers a BA or a BS degree.

_____ 3. Personal goals are not important in choosing a major.

_____ 4. A college major is a field of study.

Words from the Reading*

know   showing

*Your teacher can help you understand these words and others listed at the end of the chapter and on the Web site at http://esl.college.hmco.com/students

---

Read to find out about careers for the future.

∩ Careers for the Future

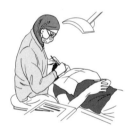

Rania, Vasyl, and Ramon know English after taking ESL classes. They have different plans and goals. There are many exciting majors at school for students who know English or are bilingual. Some careers require a short study program. Others require two or four years. Medical and dental assisting only require **on-the-job training.** Other careers, such as paramedic, dental hygienist, or computer support specialist, require an **associate degree.** A **bachelor's degree** is required for a teacher, social worker, or computer software engineer.

Rania speaks Arabic and English. She is going to be a medical assistant because she likes to help people. She starts her one-year program next year at the community college. She is going to study health, dentistry, biology, physical therapy, counseling, and English. She needs important **skills** like writing, listening, and speaking clearly. Rania is going to earn $16,700 to $27,500 per year during her career.*

Vasyl speaks Ukrainian and English. He sits in a wheelchair and doesn't have use of his legs. Vasyl is interested in computers. He is going to study at the community college for two years to be a computer support specialist. He is very confident, intelligent, and enthusiastic. He knows that he can do this job very well. Classes in computers, electronics, engineering, technology, mathematics, and English are necessary. Vasyl is very excited about his major and his future job. He is going to earn $21,300 to $48,400 per year during his career.*

Ramon likes showing other people how to do something. He is attending a community college and is studying elementary teach-

*United States Bureau of Labor Statistics

ing. He knows English and Spanish very well. After two years at the community college, he is going to transfer to the university to complete his **bachelor's degree.** Ramon is going to study mathematics, education, psychology, counseling, and English. He needs good English **skills** to become a teacher. There are many opportunities in teaching. He is going to earn $26,600 to $52,400 per year depending on where he teaches.

Rania, Vasyl, and Ramon are all very good students and have different goals for their future careers. They will each study from one to four years to reach their goal.

associate degree	a community college diploma
bachelor's degree	a university diploma
on-the-job training	learning the job by working
skill	ability

Comprehension

▶**EXERCISE 14** **Circle the number of the main idea for each paragraph.**

Paragraph 1:

1. The three students have different goals for the future.

2. There are only one-semester programs for the three students.

3. All three students are going to transfer to the university.

Paragraph 2:

1. Rania is going to study in a four-year program.

2. Rania is going to be a medical assistant.

3. Rania is going to earn $37,500 per year.

Paragraph 3:

1. Vasyl is an excellent student and is going to be a computer support specialist.

2. Vasyl is going to receive a bachelor of arts degree.

3. Vasyl is going to earn less than Rania.

Paragraph 4:

1. Ramon is attending a community college now.

2. Ramon is going to transfer to the university to complete his bachelor's degree after his community college classes.

3. Ramon is going to be a computer support specialist.

▶**EXERCISE 15** **Read the questions and answer them orally with your teacher. Then answer the questions orally with a classmate. At home, write the answers for homework. Answer in complete sentences.**

Paragraph 1:

1. What language do the three students know? _____

   _____

2. Are the programs long or short for medical and dental assistant? _____

   _____

3. Name one program that requires an associate degree. _____

   _____

4. What goals do the three students have? _____

   _____

Paragraph 2:

1. What is Rania's native language? _____

   _____

2. Why does Rania want to be a medical assistant? _____

   _____

3. How long is her study program for medical assistant? _____

   _____

4. What skills are important for Rania's career? _____

   _____

Paragraph 3:

1. What career is Vasyl interested in? _____

   _____

2. How long is the program for a computer support specialist? _____

   _____

3. What degree is Vasyl going to receive? _____

   _____

4. Is Vasyl going to do his job from a wheelchair? _____

_____

Paragraph 4:

1. What does Ramon like to show people? _____

_____

2. Where is he going to transfer after community college? _____

_____

3. What degree is he going to receive at the university? _____

_____

4. What is Ramon going to be? _____

_____

Vocabulary Practice

▶**EXERCISE 16** **Complete the sentences with words from the box**

associate degree	goals	majors	on-the-job training
program	skills	study program	transfer

1. My college offers many excellent _____.

2. After two years at the community college, I am going to _____.

3. I want an _____ from my community college.

4. Rania, Vasyl, and Ramon have important but different _____.

5. I am going to become a waiter through _____, not through classes.

6. Good English _____ are important for a teacher.

7. I want a short _____. I only want to study for one year.

8. Rania is going to take classes in a short study _____.

▶**EXERCISE 17** **Write a synonym for each <u>underlined word.</u>**

1. Ramon likes to <u>show</u> others how to do something. _____

2. There are many <u>possibilities</u> in teaching. _____

3. Rania is going to <u>make</u> $16,700 to start. _____

4. Vasyl's <u>advisor</u> tells him about certain skills. _____

5. The more education, the better <u>pay.</u> _____

6. There are many <u>programs</u> at my college. _____

 # Expansion Activity

▶Activity The Longer You Go to School   *Look at the graph, then answer the questions or complete the sentences.*

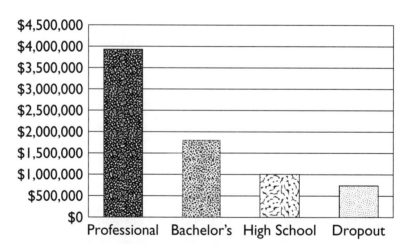

Education and Salary

Average salary per year, 25–64 years of age (based on 1999 salaries): professional degree (doctor, lawyer, etc.), $99,300 per year; bachelor of arts degree (teacher, nurse, engineer), $45,400 per year; high school diploma, $25,900 per year; high school dropout, $18,900 per year. Average lifetime salary, 25–64 years of age (based on 1999 salaries): professional degree: $3,872,700; bachelor of arts degree: $1,770,600; high school diploma: $1,010,100; high school dropout: $737,100.

Source: U.S. Census, 1999, Average Earnings by Educational Attainment

1. Which person makes the lowest pay in his or her lifetime? _____

   _____

2. If you finish high school, do you usually make more or less money than a high

   school dropout? _____

   _____

3. Does a person with a bachelor's degree make more than a high school graduate?

   _____

4. Which person earns the highest pay during his or her lifetime? _____

   _____

5. The more education you have, _____.

6. A person with a high school diploma earns more than a _____.

7. A person with a bachelor of arts degree makes more than a person with a

   _____ diploma.

8. If I earn a _____ degree, I am going to make more money than a

   person with a _____ degree.

9. The less education you have, _____.

10. I think that a person with an associate degree from a community college makes

    _____ money than a high school graduate. (Look at Reading 1,

    page 157.)

Vocabulary List

Adjectives

elderly

enthusiastic

fast-growing

on-the-job

Nouns

assisting

average

employer

lifetime

opening

skill

software

specialist

statistics

training

Careers

aerobics instructor

anesthesiologist

cleaner

computer specialist

dental assistant

dental hygienist

gardener

home health aide

hotel/motel clerk

medical assistant

registered nurse (RN)

paramedic (EMT)

petroleum engineer

restaurant worker

salesperson

sales representative

teacher's aide

Study Programs

computer science

dentistry

electronics

medicine

physical therapy

social work

technology

tele-communications

Education

high school (diploma)

community college (associate degree)

university (bachelor's, master's, doctoral degrees)

Quantitative Words

a little

a lot of

many

much

Verbs

choose

depend

going to

know

train

If you want to review vocabulary and complete additional activities related to this unit, go to the Read to Succeed 1 Web site at http://esl.college.hmco.com/students

CHAPTER II
Personal and Family Counseling

Reading I   A Professional Counselor's Job

Before You Read

▶EXERCISE I **Discuss these questions with a partner or a small group.**

1. What kinds of problems do people see a professional counselor for?

2. Is it common for people in your culture to go to a counselor?

3. How does a personal counselor help people?

▶**EXERCISE 2** **Match the pictures with the sentences below. You will use the pictures more than once.**

A.

B.

C.

1. A group session is sometimes helpful. _____

2. Some people suffer from depression. _____

3. An alcohol counselor is useful. _____

4. A counselor also helps families. _____

5. A counselor can help with drugs. _____

6. Domestic abuse is very dangerous. _____

►**EXERCISE 3** **Draw lines matching the words in column 1 with the synonyms in column 2.**

1. confidential	block
2. counselor	objective
3. goal	problem
4. issue	secret
5. obstacle	therapist

Words from the Reading*

abuse	issue
accomplish	permission
anxiety	share
clients	therapist
confidentiality	trust
depression	

*Your teacher can help you understand these words and others listed at the end of the chapter and on the Web site at http://esl.college.hmco.com/students

►**EXERCISE 4** **Scan the reading below by reading the first and last sentence of each paragraph quickly. Then answer these questions.**

Paragraph 1: What is Jill's job? _____

_____

Paragraph 2: Who does Jill help to set goals? _____

_____

Paragraph 3: Who did Jill help with issues last week? _____

_____

Paragraph 4: What part of counseling is important? _____

_____

Read about one counselor and some important parts of her job.

A Professional Counselor's Job

My name is Jill Hanks. I am a professional counselor or therapist. I help individuals and families to resolve different problems or issues in their lives. I really like my job. I help people improve their lives.

First, my clients and I set personal goals, and we try to accomplish their goals. We also identify and overcome the **obstacles** that don't let clients live their lives well. Some **obstacles** are anxiety, depression, and family and relationship problems. Other problems can be substance or sexual abuse, domestic violence, eating **disorders,** or the death of a loved one.

Last week, I was very busy helping individuals and families to **resolve** different issues. Of course, they didn't have to be "sick" to see a therapist. Some people visited me because they were unhappy, did not sleep at night, or were under stress. Other people talked to me because they wanted or tried to hurt a child or adult. I explained to all of them that difficult issues are a normal part of life.

One very important **aspect** of counseling is confidentiality. Confidentiality means I don't tell anyone the things that a client shares with me. I need the client's written permission before I give any information to someone else. The only exceptions are when the client or others are in immediate danger and when the courts say that I need to share information. My clients trust me. They know I have to protect their confidentiality or lose my license. I am glad that I help clients in this way.

aspect	part
disorder	problem
obstacle	difficulty
resolve	find a solution for

Comprehension

▶ EXERCISE 5 Write T (true) or F (false) for each statement.

_____ 1. Counselors can help only with one personal problem.

_____ 2. Jill Hanks is a medical doctor.

_____ 3. Counselors help their clients determine personal goals.

_____ 4. It is impossible to overcome life's obstacles.

_____ 5. Depression is one type of problem that people see a counselor about.

_____ 6. If a person always feels unhappy, it is a good idea to see a counselor.

_____ 7. Thoughts of hurting a person are reason to see a counselor.

_____ 8. You are sick if you see a therapist.

_____ 9. The counselor needs to protect the client's confidentiality.

_____ 10. A counselor always gives out confidential information about a client.

_____ 11. Jill works at a college and helps students choose classes.

_____ 12. Depression and family relationships are obstacles sometimes.

_____ 13. Jill's clients do not talk to her about substance abuse.

_____ 14. Some of the people that Jill saw last week were sick.

_____ 15. Aspect is the same as part.

▶**EXERCISE 6** Complete each sentence with the main idea for each paragraph.

Paragraph 1:

Jill Hanks's job as a counselor is to _____*help people find solutions to their problems*_____.

Paragraph 2:

Ms. Hanks works with her clients to _____.

Paragraph 3:

There are many _____.

Paragraph 4:

Confidentiality is _____.

Grammar Hints: Asking and answering questions in the Simple Past

▶**EXERCISE 7** Complete the sentences with the correct form of the verbs.

A. **Simple past tense of *to be:***

I was	we were
you were	you were
she was	they were

Asking and answering questions with *to be:*

Were you in class yesterday?	*Yes, I was in class.*	*No, I was not in class.*
Was Jill busy last year?	*Yes, she was busy.*	*No, she was not busy.*
Were your parents here?	*Yes, they were here.*	*No, they were not here.*

1. _____ you busy last week? Yes, I _____ busy.

2. _____ Jill sick today? No, she _____ not sick.

3. _____ your sisters at the game? Yes, they _____ at the game.

B. Simple past tense of *to do:*

I did   we did
you did   you did
he did   they did

Asking and answering questions with *to do:*

Use <u>did</u> for questions; <u>did not</u> + <u>verb</u> for negative answers.

<u>Did</u> you <u>talk</u> to her last night?	*Yes, I <u>talked</u> to her.*	*No, I <u>did not talk</u> to her.*
<u>Did</u> you <u>suggest</u> it to Jill?	*Yes, I <u>suggested</u> it to her.*	*No, I <u>did not suggest</u> it.*

1. _____ you mention it to your counselor? Yes, I _____ it.

2. _____ he need a counselor last year? No, he _____ not _____ one.

3. _____ your friends recommend a therapist? Yes, they _____ one.

4. _____ Jill help many people last week? Yes, she _____ about 10 people.

5. _____ some unhappy people visit her? Yes, a few unhappy people _____ her.

6. _____ the clients talk to Jill at home? No, they _____ not talk to her at home.

7. What _____ some people want to talk to Jill about? They _____ to her about their problems.

8. _____ Jill share her clients' information with everyone? No, she _____ not.

9. _____ Jill explain difficult issues to some clients last week? Yes, she _____ .

10. _____ Jill share information with the court last week? Yes, she _____ it.

 **Comprehension**

▶**EXERCISE 8** **Read the questions and answer them orally with your teacher. Then answer the questions orally with a classmate. At home, write the answers for homework. Answer in complete sentences.**

About the reading:

1. What is Jill Hanks's career? _____

   _____

2. What aspects of her clients' lives does Jill help them with? _____

   _____

3. What are some common problems that people see a counselor for? _____

   _____

4. When is it a good idea for a person to see a counselor? _____

   _____

5. What does confidentiality mean for a counselor? _____

   _____

6. When does the counselor need the client's permission? _____

   _____

7. When can a counselor break confidentiality? _____

   _____

Questions with *did*:

1. What did Jill do last week? *Jill helped people solve problems.*

2. What did some people wonder about?

3. What did Jill say about difficult issues?

About you:

1. When is it a good idea to see a personal counselor?

2. Why do some people not want to see a personal counselor?

3. Who helped you overcome a problem in the past?

4. What personal counseling services are there at your school?

5. What do academic counselors at your school help students with?

Vocabulary Practice

►**EXERCISE 9** **Complete the sentences with words from the box.**

A.

accomplish	depression	eating disorder	issue	resolve

1. We are going to find a solution to this problem. I know we can _____ it.

2. One thing that I want to _____ is to finish school.

3. This is a serious _____. We need to talk about it.

4. She feels sad every day, and she doesn't understand why. Her doctor thinks it is from _____.

5. He can't control his eating. Maybe he has an _____.

B.

aspect	confidentiality	overcome	set goals	therapist

1. Julia is afraid to drive, but she can _____ that by taking driving classes and practicing.

2. One important _____ about visiting another country is the interesting differences in culture.

3. If you want to reach your dreams, you have to _____ and plan what steps you need to take.

4. A counselor cannot break _____. He or she cannot tell people what the client tells him or her.

5. A good _____ listens to the client well.

C.

anxiety	client	obstacle	substance abuse	variety

1. The traffic was stopped because there was a dangerous _____ in the road.

2. Drug addiction and alcoholism are examples of _____.

3. I enjoy shopping at that bookstore because it has a big _____ of books for sale. I can find all kinds of books there.

4. _____ is the problem when the person is very anxious or afraid.

5. A personal counselor has appointments every week with the _____.

Reading 2   "Not Me! Well, Maybe . . ."

Before You Read

▶**EXERCISE 10** Draw lines matching the words in column 1 with the synonyms in column 2.

1. client	anxiety
2. depression	customer
3. stress	help
4. support	sadness

▶**EXERCISE 11** Draw lines matching the words in column 1 with the antonyms in column 2.

1. comfortable	individual
2. few	many
3. friend	negative
4. group	stranger
5. positive	uncomfortable

Read about finding a personal counselor.

"Not Me! Well, Maybe . . ."

My roommate, Jack, didn't want to talk to a counselor last year. He could not sleep. He worried a lot about his classes. He also suffered from depression for many months. I talked to him about how to find a personal counselor. He listened, but he didn't like the idea. He said, "Not me! I'm not going to see a counselor! People are going to think that I'm crazy! Pay money to talk to a stranger? Counseling didn't help my brother and his wife!"

Jack didn't understand how a counselor helps a person. I explained that a therapist is helpful in difficult times or for emotional stress. I said that a counselor is a trained professional who helps people to **discover** their personal strengths. I also mentioned that counselors emphasize the positive aspects of a person's life. I said that visiting a counselor could make a big difference in his life.

Jack asked how to find a good counselor. I said that many schools have academic and personal counselors for their students. I also suggested looking in the yellow pages of the telephone book for "Counseling Services" or "Marriage and Family Counselors" or "Mental Health Counselors." Another good idea is to talk to his doctor, friends, or **clergy.** Sometimes they know a therapist. Jack asked whether there were mental health services or crisis hotlines in our community. He wanted a **referral** for a counselor. I said that the Internet has sites with many organizations.

I reminded him, "You need to find out about the counselor and what he or she offers. Ask the counselor questions about his or her background and experience. Ask about the cost and insurance. Explain your problem and ask the counselor how he or she helps people." I suggested, "See whether you feel comfortable with this counselor. Communication is very important for your work together. You can change to another therapist if you are not comfortable. The counselor may also hold group sessions for people with similar problems. Everyone helps support each other." Jack finally decided to look for a personal counselor. He also wanted to talk to an academic counselor about his classes and problems at school.

clergy	minister, priest, rabbi
discover	find
referral	recommendation
strength	important attribute or asset

 **Comprehension**

▶**EXERCISE 12** **Write T (true) or F (false) for each statement.**

_____ 1. Counselors emphasize the negative aspects of a person.

_____ 2. A telephone book can help you find a therapist.

_____ 3. A doctor, a friend, or someone in your church can recommend a counselor.

_____ 4. The phone directory is a good place to find names and phone numbers of personal counselors.

_____ 5. Crisis hotlines cannot give referrals.

_____ 6. You should not ask too many questions when you meet a counselor.

_____ 7. The counselor needs to explain the cost for the counseling service and insurance possibilities.

_____ 8. If Jack doesn't feel comfortable with a counselor, it's best to just stop the counseling.

_____ 9. Group and individual sessions with a counselor are possible for Jack.

_____ 10. Deciding to see a counselor can be a positive change in Jack's life.

▶**EXERCISE 13** **Complete each sentence with the main idea for each paragraph.**

Paragraph 1:

Jack didn't want _____.

Paragraph 2:

A counselor is _____.

Paragraph 3:

There are many ways to _____.

Paragraph 4:

You need to know _____.

▶**EXERCISE 14** **Read the questions and answer them orally with your teacher. Then answer the questions orally with a classmate. At home, write the answers for homework. Answer in complete sentences.**

About the reading:

1. What were Jack's problems? _____

   _____

2. Did Jack like the idea of seeing a counselor? _____

   _____

3. Did Jack understand how a counselor could help him? _____

   _____

4. Are there names of counselors in the phone directory? In what section? _____

   _____

5. What services in the communities can help a person find a counselor? _____

   _____

6. Is the Internet a source for information about counselors? _____

   _____

7. What questions do clients ask a counselor when they meet? _____

_____

8. What is important between the counselor and the client? _____

_____

9. What is a group counseling session? _____

_____

10. Did Jack decide that counselors are not a good idea? _____

_____

About you:

1. Do you think counseling really helps people? _____

_____

2. What kind of counselor would you feel comfortable with? _____

_____

3. Do you know someone who has had counseling? Was it useful? _____

_____

4. Where at your school can you get information about a personal counselor? _____

_____

5. What is the name of the personal counselor at your school? What are his/her hours?

_____

_____

6. Do you have an academic counselor to help you choose a major? _____

_____

7. For a serious problem, is it better to talk to someone in your family or a counselor?

_____

_____

8. What can you do if someone is abusing your neighbor's child? _____

_____

Vocabulary Practice

▶**EXERCISE 15** **Find the words in the reading that are similar to the following words or phrases.**

1. was concerned about (¶1, line 2) _____

2. deep sadness (¶1, line 3) _____

3. Not I! (informal) (¶1, line 5–6) _____

4. advisor (¶1, line 6) _____

5. said (¶2, line 2) _____

6. therapist (¶2, line 3) _____

7. assists (¶2, line 4) _____

8. find (¶2, line 4) _____

9. capabilities (¶2, line 5) _____

10. mentioned (¶3, line 1) _____

11. priest, minister, or rabbi (¶3, line 4) _____

12. emergency counseling by phone (¶3, line 5) _____

13. recommendation (¶3, line 5) _____

14. groups (¶3, line 6) _____

15. price (¶4, line 2) _____

16. education (¶4, line 2) _____

17. talking together (¶4, line 4) _____

18. relaxed (¶4, line 5 _____

19. search (¶4, line 6) _____

▶**EXERCISE 16** **Change the meaning of the <u>underlined</u> word to its opposite. Add the prefix *dis-* or *un-*. Use a dictionary or ask your teacher if necessary.**

Prefixes

A prefix is a syllable at the beginning of a word that changes the meaning of the word. The prefixes *dis-* and *un-* mean "not." They change the meaning of a word to the opposite.

Examples: *happy / unhappy (not happy)*
            trust / distrust (not trust)

1. She is very <u>professional</u> in all her work. ____*unprofessional*____

2. I am <u>sure</u> about the answer. _____

3. This chair is <u>comfortable</u>. _____

4. The teacher is <u>satisfied</u> with the students' work. _____

5. You probably feel very <u>emotional</u> about this problem. _____

6. Do you <u>agree</u> with him? _____

7. My parents <u>approve</u> of my decision. _____

8. I know this is <u>true</u>. _____

9. I <u>like</u> listening to good news. _____

10. He was <u>worried</u> about his tests. _____

11. The man at the bank was <u>helpful</u>. _____

12. They are <u>trained</u> paramedics. _____

13. She was an <u>honest</u> person. _____

14. Nice people are <u>popular</u>. _____

15. My teacher is very <u>organized</u>. _____

16. That is a <u>true</u> story. _____

Grammar Hints: Regular past tense

▶**EXERCISE 17** Complete the sentences with the past tense form of the verbs in parentheses.

---

regular past tense, affirmative: **verb + -ed**
ask + -ed = asked   want + -ed = wanted
regular past tense, negative: **did not + present tense verb**
did not ask   did not want
I asked for an appointment last week. I did not want one this week.

---

1. I _____ (consider) going to see a doctor first.

2. He _____ (wonder) if he _____ (need) to show his insurance card.

3. The baby _____ (sleep, negative) well last night.

4. My counselor _____ (suggest) 30 minutes of exercise every day.

5. The student _____ (mention, negative) his name.

6. She _____ (explain) that she likes her job.

7. My life _____ (improve) with counseling.

8. I _____ (like, negative) the idea at first, but then I _____ (change) my mind.

Expansion Activity

▶ **Activity** **Create a Counseling Dialogue** *With a partner, write a dialogue for the following situation. Write at least five sentences for each person in the dialogue. Then present the dialogue to your classmates.*

Situation:

Two friends are talking. One has some personal problems and is feeling stressed. This person talks about how he or she feels, and the friend recommends counseling. The friend explains how to find a counselor and what happened when he or she went to see a counselor. The person who is stressed tells what he or she thinks or what he or she will do.

_____

_____

_____

_____

_____

_____

_____

_____

_____

_____

_____

_____

Vocabulary List

Adjectives

academic

comfortable

concerned

domestic

emotional

helpful

immediate

loved

negative

normal

personal

positive

professional

strange

substance

uncomfortable

Nouns

adult

anxiety / anxieties

aspect

background

clergy

client

communication

consent

danger

death

depression

disorder

group

individual

issue

license

life / lives

permission

recommendation

roommate

sadness

site

step

stranger

strength

stress / stresses

time

violence

Verbs— Present Tense

accomplish

change

discover

emphasize

feel

identify

look

lose

mean

overcome

protect

resolve

share

support

trust

Verbs— Simple Past Tense (Affirmative)

asked

considered

decided

helped

listened

reminded

said

suffered

suggested

wanted

was / were

Verbs— Simple Past Tense (Negative)

did not have

did not help

did not like

did not sleep

did not understand

did not want

Counseling Words and Phrases

confidentiality

crisis hotline

overcome obstacles

referral

resolve a problem

sessions

set personal goals

therapist

If you want to review vocabulary and complete additional activities related to this unit, go to the Read to Succeed 1 Web site at http://esl.college.hmco.com/students

CHAPTER 12

The Community

Reading 1   A New Kind of Assignment

Before You Read

▶**EXERCISE 1** Discuss these questions with a partner or a small group

1. Did you ever volunteer at a community organization?

2. Where did you volunteer?

3. What type of work do volunteer organizations do?

4. What kind of volunteer work is interesting for you?

▶**EXERCISE 2** **Listen to your teacher read each sentence. Say the sentences after your teacher. Then match each sentence with the correct picture.**

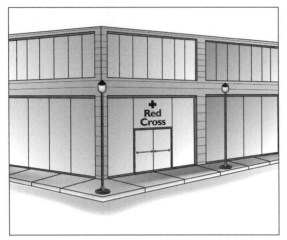

A.

B.

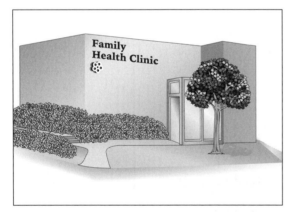

C.

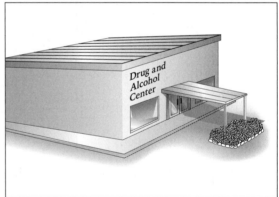

D.

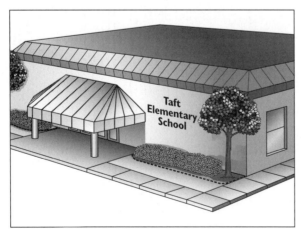

E.

F.

1. A family with no place to live can stay here. _____

2. Parents take their sick child there. _____

3. A volunteer can help children read there. _____

4. You can help very old people at this place. _____

5. An alcoholic person can find help here. _____

6. People who need emergency help go there. _____

▶**EXERCISE 3** **Write the synonym, or word with a similar meaning, for each <u>underlined</u> word or expression. Look for synonyms in the word list for the reading and in the reading.**

1. I want to <u>work for no pay</u> at a children's center. _____

2. The hard <u>work</u> our teacher gave us is due tomorrow. _____

3. The <u>type</u> of car I want costs too much money. _____

4. My class <u>donated</u> some money to the homeless shelter. _____

5. This assignment <u>seems</u> difficult but interesting. _____

6. Volunteering in the community is <u>good</u> for you. _____

7. Learning English and graduating are <u>difficult jobs</u>. _____

8. Several students <u>put up</u> their hands in class. _____

9. I <u>looked for</u> information at the library for my report. _____

10. The <u>area of medicine</u> is challenging but beneficial. _____

11. The kids are at the <u>play area</u> near the classrooms. _____

12. The <u>work</u> our teacher gave us is hard and difficult. _____

> **Words from the Reading***
>
> contribute   kind   research   volunteer
> donate   medical field   sound
>
> *Your teacher can help you understand these words and others listed at the end
>   of the chapter and on the Web site at http://esl.college.hmco.com/students

▶**EXERCISE 4** **Scan the reading below. Then answer these questions.**

1. What did Mr. Lee ask his students to do? _____

   _____

2. How did the students feel about this? _____

   _____

3. What did the students do first? _____

   _____

Read about a special assignment Mr. Lee gives his students.

∩ A New Kind of Assignment

Francisco, Paula, and Miyuki are classmates in an ESL reading class. Their teacher, Mr. Lee, gave the class a new **assignment** last week. He asked the students to volunteer two hours at a community organization. He said that this was a good **challenge** for them and a wonderful opportunity to practice English. It was a good way to meet new people and to learn about the community.

At first, Francisco felt a little nervous about this idea. He thought, In Honduras, I contributed a lot of time to my community. This is something new for me in the United States. Maybe I don't know enough English to do this. Paula was excited about the **assignment.** She didn't know anything about volunteer organizations. She **raised** her hand and asked, "Mr. Lee, what volunteer opportunities are there in this city? In Brazil, I sometimes donated my time to different projects. Once I worked with a group that built a new **playground** in a park."

Other students agreed that this project seemed difficult but **beneficial.** One student remembered that she read stories to children at a school in her hometown. Another student said that he took donations of food and clothing to low-income people. Another student taught young people in his neighborhood to play soccer twice a week. Miyuki said, "I never did this kind of work before. It sounds interesting. I want to volunteer in the medical field because I want to be a doctor." All the students wanted to explore careers. This volunteer work provided a good opportunity.

Mr. Lee saw that his students had many questions. He told them that first they needed to do research on volunteering in the community. The students divided into groups. Francisco, Miyuki, and Paula were in a group together. They made a plan and discussed it. They decided first to browse the Internet for information. They planned to telephone the nonprofit organizations that they found on the Internet. They promised to work together on everything. That afternoon, they met at the library and began to work.

assignment	work to do
beneficial	good
challenge	something difficult to try
playground	an outside place for children to play
raised	put up

Comprehension

▶**EXERCISE 5 Write T (true) or F (false) for each statement.**

_____ 1. Mr. Lee wanted the students to do an assignment that they worked on every week.

_____ 2. Mr. Lee thought that volunteering was a good way to practice English.

_____ 3. Francisco didn't feel nervous about helping in a volunteer organization.

_____ 4. Paula knew about volunteering in Brazil, but not in the United States.

_____ 5. Other students told Paula that they helped to make a playground.

_____ 6. One student read stories to children.

_____ 7. Miyuki was interested in volunteering.

_____ 8. Mr. Lee gave his students all the information about volunteering.

_____ 9. Francisco, Paula, and Miyuki made a plan for their research.

_____ 10. The three students met at the library to do research.

▶**EXERCISE 6** **Write the letter of the phrase that best completes each sentence.**

1. Mr. Lee said that _____

2. In Honduras, Francisco _____

3. Twice a week, one student _____

4. Another student _____

5. Miyuki would like _____

6. Francisco and Paula _____

7. The students met _____

8. Francisco, Paula, and Miyuki _____

9. They began to _____

10. The students were required to _____

a. did a lot of volunteer work.

b. made a plan for their project.

c. research volunteer possibilities.

d. were nervous and excited.

e. to work in the library.

f. volunteering was beneficial for the students.

g. took food and clothing to poor people.

h. was a soccer coach.

i. to work in the medical field.

j. volunteer for two hours.

▶EXERCISE 7 Complete each sentence with the main idea for each paragraph.

Paragraph 1:

Mr. Lee requested that the students _____.

Paragraph 2:

Some students had experience with volunteering in their country, but _____

_____.

Paragraph 3:

Some students had experience in volunteering, and they all _____

_____.

Paragraph 4:

The students planned _____.

▶**EXERCISE 8** **Read the questions and answer them orally with your teacher. Then answer the questions orally with a classmate. At home, write the answers for homework. Answer in complete sentences.**

About the reading:

1. What did Mr. Lee want the students to do? _____

   _____

2. What did he think the students were going to learn from the assignment? _____

   _____

3. How did Francisco feel about the assignment? _____

   _____

4. What did Paula want to know? _____

   _____

5. What volunteer experiences did other students have? _____

   _____

6. What did Miyuki think about volunteering? _____

   _____

7. What did Mr. Lee require the students to do first? _____

   _____

8. Did Paula, Miyuki, and Francisco work together? _____

   _____

9. What did Paula, Miyuki, and Francisco plan? _____

_____

10. Where did they meet? _____

_____

About you:

1. Did you ever volunteer in your native country? How was that experience? _____

_____

2. What is a good cause to donate money to? _____

_____

3. Which volunteer job is most interesting for you: helping sick or injured animals, teaching children something new, or helping senior citizens? Explain your answer.

_____

_____

📖 Vocabulary Practice

▶**EXERCISE 9** **Complete the sentences with words from the box.**

A.

challenges	clothing	donations	medical field	nervous

1. I was _____ about making phone calls in English.

2. People who work in the _____ are interested in health issues.

3. We didn't receive any _____ of blood this month.

4. A _____ store is not an example of a nonprofit organization.

5. _____ are difficult, but we learn from them.

B.

agree	browse	contribute	local	nonprofit

1. I don't _____. I have a different opinion.

2. We asked them to _____ money, but they had no money to give.

3. When you _____ the Internet, you look for information on the Internet.

4. He lives near us; he's a person from the _____ community.

5. _____ organizations are not businesses.

C.

assignment	donated	playground	raise	twice

1. When you _____ your hand in class, the teacher knows you want to say something.

2. I called him _____, but both times he didn't answer his phone.

3. This _____ will be challenging.

4. The volunteers constructed a _____ for children at the park.

5. Local businesses _____ the money for the project.

D.

catch	low-income	once	requires	research

1. He called my name to _____ my attention.

2. This job _____ a lot of energy.

3. _____ people do not have a lot of money.

4. I went to the Red Cross _____, but that was the only time.

5. You can _____ information on a variety of topics on the Internet.

▶**EXERCISE 10** **Write an antonym, or word that means the opposite, for each underlined word or expression. (Hint: Think about using the prefixes *dis-* and *un-* for some words.)**

1. Most of the students <u>agreed</u> with volunteering. _____

2. My friend was <u>interested</u> in working at a drug clinic. _____

3. One student was very <u>excited</u> about volunteering at the Red Cross.

   _____

4. Some <u>low-income</u> families donated food. _____

5. That organization <u>packs</u> medicines for other countries. _____

6. They wanted to <u>cry</u> after their car accident. _____

7. The students <u>raised</u> their hands about volunteering. _____

8. She was <u>nervous</u> about using English at the clinic. _____

Reading 2 ESL Students in the Community

Before You Read

▶**EXERCISE 11** Write the synonym, or word with a similar meaning, for each underlined word or expression. Look for synonyms in the word list for the reading.

1. We have to practice our singing for the school concert. _____

2. Please press the button on the computer mouse. _____

3. I have to choose my classes for next semester. _____

▶**EXERCISE 12** Scan the reading below. Then answer these questions.

1. In what places did the students find information? (¶1) _____

   _____

2. What did they do to prepare to call the volunteer organizations? (¶2) _____

   _____

3. What information did they learn when they called? (¶3) _____

   _____

4. What did the students find out about volunteering? (¶3) _____

   _____

Words from the Reading*

click	pack
disaster	rehearse
Internet	select

*Your teacher can help you understand these words and others listed at the end of the chapter and on the Web site at http://esl.college.hmco.com/students

ESL Students in the Community

Paula, Miyuki, and Francisco knew they had work to do to find out about volunteering in their community. They started immediately. The **librarian** showed them a book with the title *Directory of Local Nonprofit Organizations*. They found some information on how to **search** on the Internet. Miyuki typed in the words "volunteer organizations" and the name of their city. Then she clicked on the word "**search**." There was so much information! They didn't understand a lot of the articles. They copied down the names of the organizations and the phone numbers. Some community organizations had volunteer opportunities. They took down information from one site about the American Red Cross.

Three hours later, the three students were more **confident,** and they had enough information. They met and selected three organizations to call. Miyuki chose a disaster relief organization. Paula planned to call the local art museum. Francisco wanted to contact an afterschool sports program for elementary school children. The students talked about what questions to ask. They practiced the questions and corrected each other's pronunciation. They laughed at their mistakes. They **postponed** the phone calls until their next meeting. They rehearsed the phone calls with Mr. Lee the next day.

Paula, Miyuki, and Francisco telephoned the organizations the next day. They were very surprised at all the work that the organizations did. The person who answered the phone at a disaster relief organization explained that volunteers helped in many ways. They packed medical supplies for disaster areas. They **sorted** dry and canned food and clothing for people in need. In case of an earthquake, hurricane, or other natural disaster, volunteers gave out supplies to people left homeless. Volunteers also assisted people staying in temporary shelters. The art museum also needed volunteers. Volunteers helped **mail** out information about the museum events and gave information to visitors. Volunteers at the afterschool program read to children and taught them a sport or art. They spent time with children of working parents. There were so many possibilities. The students were going to learn and report a lot to their class. Volunteering was going to be a great adventure!

confident	sure
librarian	person who works in the library
mail	letters and packages; send letters or packages
postpone	wait to do later
search	look for
sort	organize

Comprehension

▶EXERCISE 13 Write T (true) or F (false) for each statement.

_____ 1. There was no one to help the students at the library.

_____ 2. They used the words "volunteer organizations" and the search button to help them find information on the Internet.

_____ 3. The students understood all the information they read on the Internet.

_____ 4. The students had no problems in the library.

_____ 5. Francisco wanted to call an afterschool program.

_____ 6. The students practiced calling the nonprofits for information.

_____ 7. Volunteers in disaster relief organizations only answer the phone.

_____ 8. Children in afterschool programs spend time with the volunteers.

_____ 9. Volunteers at the art museum give information to museum visitors.

_____ 10. Volunteering doesn't offer many possibilities.

▶EXERCISE 14 Complete each sentence with the main idea for each paragraph.

Paragraph 1:

At the library, the students _____.

Paragraph 2:

Before making the phone calls, the students _____.

Paragraph 3:

Volunteers can _____.

▶**EXERCISE 15** **Read the questions and answer them orally with your teacher. Then answer the questions orally with a classmate. At home, write the answers for homework. Answer in complete sentences.**

About the reading:

1. What did the librarian show the students? _____

   _____

2. Where did the students search on the Internet? _____

   _____

3. What did the students copy down? _____

   _____

4. What organization did Miyuki choose? _____

   _____

5. What did they practice and correct? _____

   _____

6. What did they rehearse? _____

   _____

7. What work did the volunteers do at the disaster relief organization? _____

   _____

About you:

1. Do you have experience using the Internet? How do you use the Internet? _____

   _____

2. Do you have time to volunteer? _____

   _____

3. What are some difficulties that ESL students can have with volunteering? _____

   _____

📖 Vocabulary Practice

▶**EXERCISE 16 Complete the sentences with words from the box**

A.

| click | find out | freezes | get to work | helpful |

1. He always assists the customers as much as he can; he is very _____.

2. We need to start working on this! We need to _____.

3. I called the school to _____ information on their programs.

4. When you use the computer, you need to _____ on the button.

5. My computer is broken. It often _____ when I'm working on it.

B.

| confident | offer | postpone | search | select |

1. When I volunteer at an organization, I _____ any help they can use.

2. We can't do this now; we need to _____ it for later.

3. You need to choose one place to go. Which one do you want to _____?

4. I am _____ that you will like it.

5. Every time I lose my keys, I _____ for them for hours.

C.

| adventure | librarian | mail | pack | rehearse |

1. The students had to _____ their questions. The practice was very necessary.

2. We helped to _____ the books into boxes.

3. A _____ is trained to help people find information.

4. Life is full of _____. You don't know what is going to happen next.

5. I'm waiting for a letter to arrive. The _____ will be here soon.

▶**EXERCISE 17** **Write a synonym for each <u>underlined</u> word.**

1. Before volunteering, the students <u>organized</u> their notes. _____

2. They <u>looked over</u> the Internet sites for organizations. _____

3. Mr. Lee <u>suggested</u> two volunteer organizations. _____

4. We <u>gave away</u> some clothing to the homeless shelter. _____

5. My group <u>got together</u> at my house to study. _____

6. I <u>practiced</u> several hours for my volunteer interview. _____

7. We <u>talked to</u> three organizations by telephone. _____

8. My classmate was so <u>stressed</u> about her interview. _____

9. I <u>pressed</u> the computer mouse to open the volunteer site. _____

10. Each student had to <u>choose</u> a topic for the reports. _____

▶**EXERCISE 18** **In the blank space write an antonym for the <u>words to the right</u> of the sentence. Use the prefixes dis-, un-, and in- before the word if necessary.**

1. The students had to _____ the medical supplies. <u>unpack</u>

2. I was very _____ during my interview. <u>nervous and shy</u>

3. The answer he gave in class was _____. <u>incorrect</u>

4. Miyuki _____ when she saw the homeless children. <u>laughed</u>

5. We are very _____ about where to volunteer. <u>decided</u>

6. The _____ program at the grammar school is perfect. <u>before school</u>

7. Volunteers helped in _____ ways at the organization. <u>a few</u>

8. Some students were _____ about the assignment. <u>bored</u>

9. Two students _____ in class about the assignment. <u>agreed</u>

10. Most students agreed that volunteering was _____. <u>a waste of time</u>

Grammar Hints: Irregular Past Tense

The irregular past tense of verbs varies. You have to learn their forms. Here are a few examples.

Present	Past
feel	felt
find	found
give	gave

▶**EXERCISE 19** **Complete the sentences with the past tense form of the verbs in parentheses. Use your dictionary or ask your teacher if necessary.**

1. My instructor _____ (teach) four classes last semester.

2. He _____ (give) me an "A" on the test.

3. I _____ (leave) my name and phone number with the volunteer coordinator.

4. We _____ (make) the decision to work together.

5. They _____ (find, negative) any information.

6. They _____ (think, negative) it was difficult to do research.

7. The students _____ (sit) in groups.

8. They _____ (choose) an organization to volunteer in.

9. Sara _____ (feel) nervous about using a computer.

10. I _____ (write, negative) any notes about that organization.

Expansion Activity

▶ Activity   Where Can I Volunteer?   *Research a local volunteer organization that interests you. On your own or with one or more classmates, visit the organization and find out the volunteer opportunities available. Report about your research to your class.*

Vocabulary List

Adjectives

afterschool

beneficial

canned

dry

low-income

temporary

wonderful

Nouns

adventure

assignment

challenge

classmate

disaster

field

homeless

information

Internet

librarian

mail

meeting

organization

playground

possibility / possibilities

project

relief

research

supply / supplies

Community Agencies

alcohol clinic

drug clinic

health clinic

homeless shelter

Red Cross

Salvation Army

senior center

Verbs— Present Tense

agree

assist

browse

click

contact

contribute

copy

correct

decide

donate

laugh

mail

meet

pack

postpone

raise

rehearse

search

select

sort

type

understand

volunteer

Verbs— Irregular Past Tense

choose / chose

feel / felt

find / found

freeze / froze

give / gave

have / had

know / knew

leave / left

lose / lost

make / made

say / said

sit / sat

take / took

teach / taught

tell / told

think / thought

write / wrote

If you want to review vocabulary and complete additional activities related to this unit, go to the Read to Succeed 1 Web site at http://esl.college.hmco.com/students

Appendix

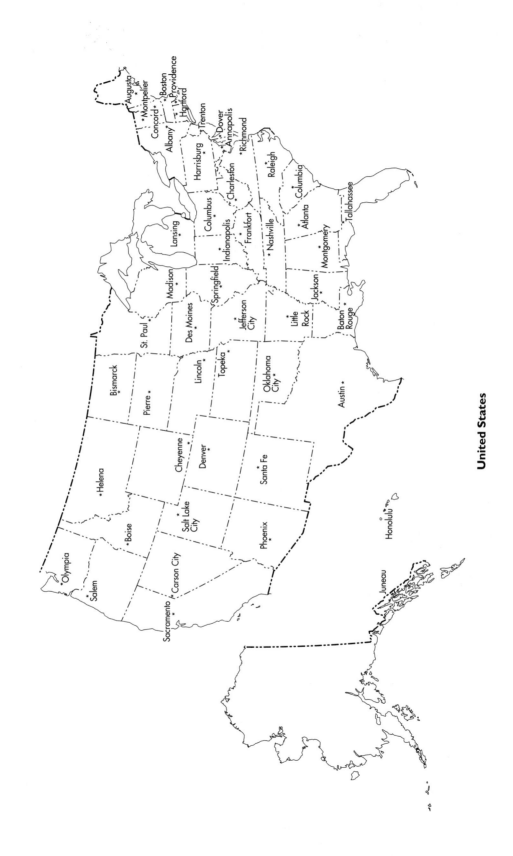

The World

MY Thank You BOOK

© MCMLXII, The Standard Publishing Company

a FRANCES HOOK picture book

with stories by WANDA HAYES

© MCMLXIV, The STANDARD PUBLISHING Company ● Cincinnati, Ohio ● Printed in U.S.A.

God Gave Me
Mother and Daddy

Thank you, Mother, for washing my face.
Umm! The soap smells good.
Thank you for putting my Sunday clothes on me.
I'll stand still for you.
Thank you for combing my hair.
Now I'm ready for breakfast.

Thank you, Daddy, for helping me put on my nice,
    warm coat.
I can button two buttons.
Thank you for wrapping my red scarf around my neck,
    and for snapping my cap under my chin, where it
    tickles.
Thank you for putting my mittens on my hands.
Now they won't get cold.

Thank you, God, for the church house and for my
    teacher.
Thank you 'cause Mother and Daddy take me to church
    with them.
Thank you for Mother and Daddy.

God Gave Me Berries

Good, red strawberries!
Daddy and I picked them from a bush.
Daddy showed me the ones that were ripe, and I pulled
  them by the green part and put them in a basket.

Mommy washed the strawberries in cold water.
I like to hold them by the stem and bite the red part.
Berries are sweet, and juice runs down my chin;
And sometimes it gets on my hands.

I throw the green parts of the berries away, but I eat
  all the red parts.
Then I wash my hands.
My mouth still tastes like berries, and my tongue is
  very red.

Thank you, God, for berries.

God Gives Me Food

One time when Jesus was teaching a crowd of people, He said, "Look at the birds that fly in the air. They do not plant food and put it into barns, but your heavenly Father feeds them. And you are worth more than birds.

"Do not worry about whether you will have something to eat and something to drink. Your heavenly Father knows everything you need."

Story from Matthew 6:25, 26, 31, 32

Heavenly Father,
    Thank you for food
That my mother fixes
    (It tastes very good):
A tall glass of milk,
    Cold and white,
My bowl full of cereal
    (I eat every bite),
Meat and vegetables,
    Soft mashed potatoes,
Butter and bread,
    Sweet, red tomatoes,
And cake and ice cream
    (A very nice treat);
Thank you for everything
    I like to eat.
                    Amen.

God Gave Me Clothes

My daddy gave me a new coat for my birthday.
I'm a year older now.
My coat is brown and soft like my teddy bear.

"Now put this arm in," Daddy said.
"Now this one."
The coat felt funny. It was crooked.
But Daddy fixed it. He buttoned each button—
    one, two, three, four, five buttons.

Then Daddy and I looked in the big mirror.
I liked my new coat.
I laughed, and Daddy laughed too.
Then he gave me a big hug around the middle.

"Thank you, Daddy, for my coat."

God Gave Me Toys

I like to play with my toys.
I like to play house.
I sit in my rocking chair
   and rock my baby doll to sleep.
Then I put her in bed and sing a little song to her
   like the one Mommy sings to me.

Sometimes I like to play zoo.
I pretend each one of my animals is in a cage.
Then baby doll and I go to the zoo
   and look at each animal.
I say, "Grrr!" for my kitty
   and pretend she is a big lion.
And baby doll and I hurry past the elephant's cage
   so he won't squirt water on us
   with his big, gray trunk.

Pretending is lots of fun,
   but do you know what I like to do best of all?
I like to play with my friends,
   Bobby, and Susan, and Rachel.
Toys are the most fun when we all play together.

God Gave Me Flowers

One day Mommy and I planted little brown things called bulbs. We planted them in the soft dirt by our house. Mommy said, "After a while we shall have pretty flowers in our yard."

Every day I looked outside at the ground. And every day all I saw was dark brown dirt. Sometimes the rain came down and made mud. Then the sun shone and dried the mud and made it dirt again.

"When will we have pretty flowers in our yard, Mommy?"

"In a few more days," she said. "Flowers need plenty of water and sunshine before they are ready to grow."

One day I saw something green sticking up out of the ground. "Is that a flower?" I asked Mommy.

"No, it is a leaf. Soon we shall have flowers."

Every day I looked. Every day the leaf was taller. Every day Mommy said, "Our flowers will grow."

After breakfast one day, Mommy said, "Look in the yard today. Look where we planted the bulbs."

I did look. Do you know what I saw? Flowers! Yellow flowers were on the ends of the tall, green leaves.

"They are pretty," I said.

"Yes," said Mother. "God made the pretty yellow flowers to grow for you."

God Gave Me Rain

"Plop—zip! Plop—zip!" The rain makes a funny sound on my umbrella. Each drop goes "plop," then it rolls down my silky umbrella, "zip." From underneath it looks like a lot of tiny rivers running down the top of my umbrella.

Raindrops run right off my raincoat. It's slippery, and they slide right off. Sometimes little drops of water stay on the back of my hands. And they are hard to shake off.

"Splash! Splash!" go my boots when I walk in a little puddle. If I splash too hard, water gets inside my boots. Wet socks don't feel good, and Mommy doesn't like them either.

Sometimes I move the toe of one boot back and forth slowly in the water. "Swish. Swish."

Rain is pretty. It's red on my umbrella, on my raincoat, and on my boots. It's green on the grass, and gray on the sidewalk. It's all different colors in the puddles. And after it stops raining, little drops of water on grass and leaves shine like diamonds.

Rain makes everything outside smell good.

Thank you, God, for the rain.

God Gave Me Bible School

I like to go to Bible school. My kind teacher smiles and says, "Come in. You look very pretty today." Then I put my money in the basket. That is how we say, "I love you, God."

I like to go to Bible school. Every Sunday I get to see Paula and Billy and Freddie and Roger. But sometimes one of us is sick.

Sometimes we look at pictures on the table. The one I like best is a picture of Jesus.

We sing and pray and listen to Teacher tell us a story from God's Book. One time he told us that Jesus put mud on a blind man's eyes and made him see again. We looked at a picture of Jesus and the blind man. Teacher said, "Aren't you glad God gave us Jesus?"

"Yes," we said. Then we closed our eyes and prayed, "Thank you, God, for Jesus,"

And I said in my head where no one else can hear, "Thank you, God, for my teacher and for Bible school. Amen."

God Gave Me My Dog

I have a little puppy named Sandy. I show Sandy I love him by patting his head and rubbing his neck. His hair feels soft and smooth. Sandy likes for me to pat him.

I take good care of Sandy. I give him good dog food and plenty of water. I play with him and fix his bed for him. Sandy likes that.

When I take care of Sandy, he licks my face and wags his tail.

When someone does something for me, I say "Thank you."

Licking my face and wagging his tail is how Sandy says "Thank you."

Thank you, God, for my dog Sandy.

God Gave Me Birds

One day my mother said, "Come and look out the window, but be very quiet." So I walked on my tiptoes over to the window with Mother. She put a finger over her mouth. "Shhh," she said. And she pointed outside to the tree in our back yard.

There on a big, black branch was a little round dish made out of dry grass. Mother whispered, "That's a bird's nest. Look at the mother bird feeding her babies."

The little baby birds must have been very hungry because they opened their mouths very wide and made a lot of noise. "Chirp! Chirp! Chirp!" And the mother bird gave each baby bird a worm to eat.

Mother said, "God makes sure that every bird has food to eat."

And God gives me food too.

Thank you, God, for taking care of the birds and for taking care of me.

God Gave Me Squirrels

A friendly, fuzzy little squirrel
   Lives high up in a tree.
I watch him from my window,
   But he never looks at me.

When summertime is nearly gone,
   And leaves begin to fall,
My squirrel friend takes nuts to his tree—
   He holds them in his jaw.

He hides them carefully in a hole
   Where only squirrels can go;
He has to hide them now, before
   The ground is white with snow.

So all year long the squirrel has food
   For all his family.
God takes care of friendly squirrels
   And children just like me.

God Gave Me Day

Thank you, God, for mornings
    when I can wake up and wash my face
    and put clean clothes on, all by myself.

Thank you for mornings
    when Mommy gives me a big hug and kiss and says,
    "Good morning, dear. What would you like for
    breakfast?"

And thank you for the fun I have playing with my doll
    and with my friends outside in the daytime.

Thank you for the pretty blue sky,
    and the yellow sunshine,
    and the flowers that smell so good,
    and for the bees that hum, "Bzzzz. Bzzzz."

Thank you for afternoons when Daddy comes home.
Thank you, God,
    for everything that makes me happy all day long.

God Gave Me Night

When I look out the window at night,
   the sky is dark, dark blue and the sun is all gone.
That's so we can sleep.

I see a big, white, shiny moon
   that looks like a big, smiling face.
Sometimes the moonlight shines right in the window.
I can see it on the floor,
   and when I put my hand down to touch it,
   the moonlight shines on me.

Everywhere I look in the sky,
   there are little white stars that sparkle.

Sometimes I put my eyes right next to the window
   and look just as far as I can into the sky.
And I know that God is up there
   'way past the stars, the moon, and everything.
God is up there where no one can see Him,
   but where He can see everyone.
And He's taking care of people 'way down here.

God Gave Me Bed

When night comes and it's dark outside, and I'm sleepy and start to yawn, my mother helps me get ready for bed.

I take a bath and splash a little and have fun. Mommy dries me with a big towel that almost covers me up. She puts good-smelling powder on me, and I climb into my soft, warm pajamas. They feel so-o-o good!

After I run and kiss Daddy good night, I get down on my knees beside my bed and talk to God. I say "Thank you" to God for Mother and Daddy and all the good times I've had that day.

Mommy pulls back the covers on my bed, and I hurry and climb in with my teddy bear. Then Mommy covers me up to my neck and tucks some covers under my feet.

Mommy kisses me good night, and I hug her and kiss her real big. Then Mommy turns out the light.

That's when teddy and I go to sleep until the morning.

Thank you, God, for my nice soft bed and pillow.

God Gave Me Arms

God gave me arms
   to hug my mother and daddy
   and my puppy and my dolly.
God gave me arms to carry folded towels for my mother.
God gave me arms to fold when I'm in church.

God gave me hands to clap when I'm happy.
God gave me hands to rub my daddy's cheek;
   sometimes it's smooth,
   and sometimes it has whiskers.
God gave me hands to give my offering to Jesus.

God gave me fingers to hold my spoon so I can eat.
God gave me fingers to pick a pretty flower
   for my teacher.
God gave me fingers to fold together when I pray,
   "Thank you, God, for everything. Amen."

All Things Bright and Beautiful

Cecil Alexander · Imogene Humphrey

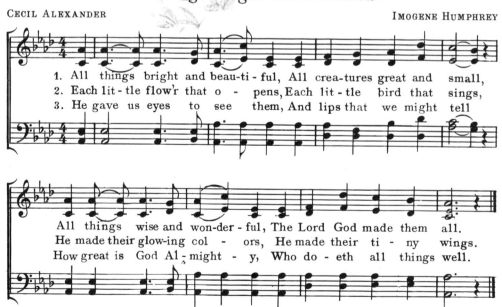

1. All things bright and beau-ti-ful, All crea-tures great and small,
2. Each lit-tle flow'r that o - pens, Each lit-tle bird that sings,
3. He gave us eyes to see them, And lips that we might tell

All things wise and won-der-ful, The Lord God made them all.
He made their glow-ing col - ors, He made their ti - ny wings.
How great is God Al - might - y, Who do - eth all things well.